Spreading Activation, Lexical Priming and the Semantic Web

Michael Pace-Sigge

Spreading Activation, Lexical Priming and the Semantic Web

Early Psycholinguistic Theories, Corpus Linguistics and AI Applications

palgrave
macmillan

Michael Pace-Sigge
Department of English Language
    and Culture
University of Eastern Finland
Joensuu, Finland

ISBN 978-3-319-90718-5   ISBN 978-3-319-90719-2   (eBook)
https://doi.org/10.1007/978-3-319-90719-2

Library of Congress Control Number: 2018940750

Cover illustration: © Stephen Bonk/Fotolia.co.uk

Printed on acid-free paper

This Palgrave Pivot imprint is published by the registered company Springer International
Publishing AG part of Springer Nature
The registered company address is: Gewerbestrasse 11, 6330 Cham, Switzerland

ACKNOWLEDGEMENTS

My thanks go to the following people:

Michael Hoey, who got me interested into corpus linguistics and, in particular, the theory of lexical priming;

Mike O'Donnell, Paul Rayson and Gerold Schneider, with whom I had a number of enlightening conversations with regard to computational linguistics and the use of machine learning for linguistics;

Allan Collins, Peter Norvig and Yorick Wilks, who took time off their busy schedule to e-mail back answers to my naïve questions;

All the people at Palgrave Macmillan, in particular my editor, Beth Farrow, as well as the copy readers and the anonymous reviewers who enabled me to proceed.

My particular thanks go to Jess Pope, Katie J. Patterson and Karl-Hermann Wieners, who diligently read the draft version of the text and helped to correct and clarify a number of issues. All remaining errors are, of course, mine.

My particular thanks and the book's dedication go to Katie, for initiating this project and encouraging me all the way.

To Mr. "Hops" van Carrot, in memory.

CONTENTS

LIST OF FIGURES

LIST OF TABLES

Languages are complex, random, contingent biological processes that are subject to the whims of evolution and cultural change. What constitutes a language is not an eternal ideal form, represented by the settings of a small number of parameters, but rather is the contingent outcome of complex processes. Since they are contingent, it seems they can only be analyzed with probabilistic models. Since people have to continually understand the uncertain. ambiguous, noisy speech of others, it seems they must be using something like probabilistic reasoning (Norvig 2011).

CHAPTER 1

Introduction

Abstract The aim of the book is to provide an overview of the intercon-
nection of linguistics and artificial intelligence (AI). By the late 1950s,
researchers seriously considered tools to teach machines to comprehend
human language. Thus, engineers in the computing sciences started working together with linguists. Today, trillions of words from different sources
can be collated and used for computer-based calculations. This allows for a
better-informed (because fully empirical) vision of language. As a result, it
can be seen that linguistic knowledge underpins the ability of a computational device to process human language. Conversely, such electronic devices
are getting closer to creating a mirror image of how language is processed,
thus providing support for theories of the underlying structure of language.

Keywords Turing · Quillian · Norvig · Spreading activation · AI

It was in the early 1960s, on a wave of progress and optimistic faith in
technological solutions, that everything seemed to come together. The
first automated computing machines were not much over a decade old
when researchers seriously considered tools to teach these machines
to comprehend human language. Thus, engineers in the computing
sciences started working together with linguists. Ideas, even good ideas,
need incubation time, however. Other people have to work on these
ideas, coming up with new techniques; new people might think of new

© The Author(s) 2018   1
M. Pace-Sigge, *Spreading Activation,*
Lexical Priming and the Semantic Web,
https://doi.org/10.1007/978-3-319-90719-2_1

applications for the same idea but in very different fields. It is a bit like the first steps of human bipeds to leave the ground they were standing on. Apart from special geographical features (like hills and mountains), all man could see was their surrounds. The moment a balloon took people up into the air, however, a completely new view of the familiar surroundings was possible. Similarly, modern technology allows us to delve into subatomic geographies. The same experience is true when going beyond the use of single books as a basis to understand and manipulate language. With the second decade of the second millennium approaching, trillions of words from different sources can be collated and used for computer-based calculations—with tools that are available to most people who have nothing more than a simple PC or mobile device with the appropriate application. This then allows a new, different, better-informed (because fully empirical) vision of language. Yet it is much more than that—this knowledge can now be harvested to have machine-mediated understanding of spoken utterances; algorithms can now be designed to mimic natural human speech. As a result, we are witnessing a whole new dimension in communication.[1]

Consequently, a parallel set of conclusions can be drawn: it can be seen that linguistic knowledge underpins the ability of a computational device to process human language in written or spoken form. Conversely, such electronic devices are getting closer and closer in creating a mirror image to how language is produced, processed and understood thus providing support for the theories of the underlying structure of language, while undermining rival claims: if a form of AI works, this can be seen as a result of successfully turning one theory into practise.

The genesis of the book is a story of coincidental discoveries which, over time, have built up to draw connections that changed the intended outcome several times. While I was preparing my first book, Lexical Priming in Spoken English (Pace-Sigge 2013), I happened to read Steven Levy's 2011 book about the search engine company, Google. As an aside, Levy encourages the readers to have a look at the personal page of Google's first head of research, Peter Norvig (2017)—to see something devoid of gimmicks: a proper engineer's web page. Curious, I went and had a look, only to find that Norvig himself had made, in a number of his published articles, reference to Ross Michael Quillian—the very man that I had identified in my book as a key figure in the development of the concept of *priming*. Looking at the processes to retrieve the best possible search results for any given Google search, as described by Levy, the connection to the concept of *lexical priming* became quite obvious. This connection has subsequently been described, albeit not in too much detail, in my earlier book.

A few years down the line, my partner suggested I could write a primer on the concept of lexical priming as part of the Palgrave Pivot series. It took, however, another year or two before I had time to think about that project. Yet, as I started to investigate the matter, it became clear that a far more interesting project offered itself: the link between the psycholinguistic theory of *lexical priming* developed by Michael Hoey (2005) and the current developments in speech recognition and speech production technology which are born out of current advances in AI. For both appear to have a common root in the concepts of the *semantic web* and *spreading activation*, first developed by Quillian. The task for Quillian (1969) was to create a theoretical framework explaining how to programme a machine to understand natural human speech—the *Teachable Language Comprehender* (*TLC*) as he called it. The core to this task was, for Quillian, to create a form of *Word-Sense Disambiguation* (*WSD*). Tellingly, research into what is now referred to as *WSD* is at the heart of many AI and computational linguistics projects in the twenty-first century.[2] As a consequence, it seems to make sense to write a book that shows the development of the theory, then outline the two strands of research which developed out of it and finally see what these two communities of researchers can learn from each other.

There are, of course, a number of hugely important books available that cover the concepts in this book in far greater detail. First and foremost, the magisterial bible on AI, Stuart Russell's and Peter Norvig's *Artificial Intelligence. A modern approach*. Originally published in late 1995, the latest updated edition came out in 2016. The book more focussed on the area discussed here—language—is the equally impressive *Speech and Language Processing: An Introduction to Natural Language Processing, Computational Linguistics and Speech Recognition* by Daniel Jurafsky and James H. Martin. Its first edition was published in 2000, with the second edition announced for 2018. One might want to take a shortcut—as the publisher, Prentice Hall (now Pearson) must have thought—and go for the 2014 book *Speech and Language Processing* by Jurafsky, Martin, Norvig and Russell. All three books weigh in at the 1000 page mark, so, if pressed for time, people might just want to have a look at Cambria's and White's *Jumping NLP Curves: A Review of Natural Language Processing Research* (2014) which is an article a mere ten pages in length. Shorter still is the article in *Science* by Julia Hirschberg and Christopher D. Manning, simply called *Advances in Natural Language Processing*, which is succinct, uses helpful graphics and packs the latest research of (2015) into five three-columned pages. Similarly, Steven Abney's (1996) article *Statistical Methods and Linguistics* works as a helpful primer. For those who learn about *Lexical Priming*, there is Michael Hoey's 2005 book of the same name which serves as the best possible introduction to the topic.

Throughout the book, a number of examples will be given. More often than not, these are based on "naturally occurring texts"—that is material taken from published books or corpora—like the BNC or my own collection of spoken corpora. Where concordance lines have been investigated, collocations compared or frequencies investigated, the *Wordsmith 7* (Scott 2017) has been used.

This short book is divided into five chapters: there is the *Introduction*—the chapter at hand. This is followed by a second chapter where a brief history of AI theories will be given—the thoughts of Alan Turing and his predecessors. The focus is on the work of Ross M. Quillian, his early collaborator, Allan Collins (cf. Collins and Quillian, 1969), and the resulting work by like-minded researchers who developed the key concepts discussed in this book, namely *priming, spread-activation* and the *semantic web*. Chapter 3 provides a platform to showcase the more recent developments that have grown out of the early groundwork laid. On the one hand, there are the latest theories in the field of linguistics. These are based on empirical data taken from naturally occurring language, namely the *lexical priming theory* and how it can be used to explain structures of language that corpus linguists have uncovered. On the other hand, there are the technical applications in the form of the development of evermore sophisticated algorithms that also deal with the use of language. Here, the focus will be on key achievements in the 1980s by IBM which prepared a solid foundation for applications that are now widely used in mobile and desktop devices—namely "assistants" like Amazon's *Alexa*, Apple's *SIRI* or Google's (and Android's) *Google Go* (*Google Assistant*).

Chapter 4 starts with showing that many key players in the AI community have deep roots in linguistic research. This is then followed with a brief overview of those topics that have seen a lot of research undertaken by linguists—yet there is little or no work by NLP engineers to address these issues which are crucial for language production and understanding. The chapter ends with a vista of possible future research, and collaboration will be presented. The book is completed by a short *Conclusion* which reviews some of the key points made here.

NOTES

1. It does not end with this spoken or written human-to-machine interaction either. Barfield (2015) describes how brainwaves can be "read". This kind of technology clearly caught Facebook's eye who, in their 2017 developer conference, announced that in future users can "like" posts through having their thought processes read. Given the possible implications of such a technology, this might be deemed, however, as too terrifying a prospect.
2. Ironically, the whole process seems to have come full circle, as AI developers who describe the concept of spreading activation reference me as to the beginnings of the concept. This meant that, during the research for this book, I came across a paper by an IBM *Watson* developer (Mac an tSaoir 2014) where I found my own book cited.

REFERENCES

Abney, Steve. 1996. Statistical Methods and Linguistics. In *The Balancing Act: Combining Symbolic and Statistical Approaches to Language*, ed. Judith L. Klavans and Philip Resnik. Cambridge: MIT Press.

Barfield, Woodrow. 2015. *Cyber-Humans: Our Future with Machines*. Cham: Springer.

Cambria, Erik, and Bebo White. 2014. Jumping NLP Curves: A Review of Natural Language Processing Research. *IEEE Computational Intelligence Magazine* 9 (2): 48–57.

Collins, Allan M., and M. Ross Quillian. 1969. Retrieval Time from Semantic Memory. *Journal of Verbal Learning and Verbal Behaviour* 8 (2): 240–248.

Hirschberg, Julia, and Christopher D. Manning. 2015. Advances in Natural Language Processing. *Science* 349 (6245): 261–266.

Hoey, Michael. 2005. *Lexical Priming: A New Theory of Words and Language*. London: Routledge.

Jurafsky, Daniel, and James H. Martin. 2000. *Speech and Language Processing: An Introduction to Natural Language Processing, Computational Linguistics and Speech Recognition*. Englewood Cliffs: Prentice Hall.

Jurafsky, Daniel, James H. Martin, Peter Norvik, and Stuart Russell. 2014. *Speech and Language Processing*. Englewood Cliffs: Prentice Hall.

Levy, Steven. 2011. *In the Plex: How Google Thinks, Works and Shapes Our Lives*. New York: Simon & Schuster.

Mac an tSaoir, Rónan. 2014. Using Spreading Activation to Evaluate and Improve Ontologies. *COLING*, 2237–2248.

Norvig, Peter. 2017. peternorvig.com. Last Accessed 09/2017.

Pace-Sigge, Michael. 2013. *Lexical Priming in Spoken English Usage.* Houndmills, Basingstoke: Palgrave Macmillan.

Quillian, M. Ross. 1969. The Teachable Language Comprehender: A Simulation Program and Theory of Language. *Computational Linguistics* 12 (8) (August): 459–476.

Russell, Stuart, and Peter Norvig. 1995. *Artificial Intelligence: A Modern Approach.* Englewood Cliffs: Prentice Hall.

Scott, M. 2017. *WordSmith Tools Version 7.* Stroud: Lexical Analysis Software.

CHAPTER 2

M. Ross Quillian, Priming, Spreading-Activation and the Semantic Web

Abstract This provides a brief history of artificial intelligence theories—in particular, the theories of Alan Turing and his predecessors. Early thoughts how language processes in a human mind can be replicated in a language-learning machine will be shown here. The focus of the chapter is the work of M. Ross Quillian, who developed the key concepts discussed in this book, namely *priming, spreading activation* and the *semantic web* and how these can facilitate access to the *semantic memory*. Quillian describes his creation as "a simulation program"—that is a program that can be taught to understand (process) language. Importantly, it was also meant to be a "theory of language".

Keywords Quillian · Spreading activation · Priming · Semantic web Semantic memory

2.1 Computational Groundwork

There are a large number of publications which will tell the reader about the roots of artificial intelligence. Some trace the philosophy back to Aristotle, others (including Turing 1950) say that this development started with the computing machine Charles Babbage designed in the nineteenth century (but did not have the technology to actually build). It appears, however, to be the discussions to providing mathematical

© The Author(s) 2018
M. Pace-Sigge, *Spreading Activation,*
Lexical Priming and the Semantic Web,
https://doi.org/10.1007/978-3-319-90719-2_2

solutions to decisions-making problems in the twentieth century that really created a foundation for what was to become *artificial intelligence research*. McCulloch and Pitts (1943) are early proponents of "neural networks" as their contribution to the question posed by Hilbert in 1900, namely whether there exists an algorithm for deciding the truth of any logical proposition involving the natural numbers. This became known as the *Entscheidungsproblem*—the problem of deciding whether the criteria for "truth" are met. This is an issue that has been discussed at great length by philosophers, amongst whom Ludwig Wittgenstein is probably most relevant here. He wrote:

> Or, again, what, at any stage we are to call "being in accord" with that sentence (and with the meaning you then put into the sentence — whatever that may have consisted in). It would almost be more correct to say, not that an intuition was needed at every stage, but that a new decision was needed at every stage. (Wittgenstein /186/1953)

Following in the footsteps of Kurt Gödel, Alan Turing said that, in logic, there are some *true statements* that cannot be decided by any algorithm. Thus, Turing (1937a, b) sets out to describe a system that provides computability of "to the intuitive idea of 'effective calculability'": providing the space where calculations are possible. With this, he links his work with those of the American mathematician Alonzo Church.[1] Famously, the so-called Turing Test was described in 1950 in a paper that provocatively started with the following words:

> I propose to consider the question, 'Can machines think?' This should begin with the definitions of the meaning of the terms 'machine' and 'think'. The definitions might be framed so as to reflect so far as possible the normal use of the words, but this attitude is dangerous. (Turing 1950: 433)

It is a wonderfully readable paper (unlike his mathematical research papers), and it is here that Turing points out that it is the question-and-answer method (in any field the interrogator sees fit) which seems to be best suited to demonstrate intelligence.[2] Crucially, Turing speaks of these digital computers as *learning machines*—indicating a move away from the static Turing machine which will only be able to fulfil the commands it has been programed to undertake. Better still, these learning machines will have mechanisms that work, in fact, similar to the human mind. He says that an important feature must be that the teacher will mostly be unaware about how and what has been "learned" (though the teacher may predict what is happening). This points towards a high degree of autonomy of the digital automaton. And, while human fallibility will be reduced, the learning process cannot, according to Turing, be one hundred per cent certain (as the question is whether the machine could unlearn in that case what it has wrongly acquired). As a possible solution, the introduction of a random element is proposed. These last two points are rather crucial when we look at present-day AI machines, because it is still the human side of the equation that decides what machines learn. The results might be embarrassingly wrong headed— but this only reflects that this part of Turing's envisioned digital intelligence is not yet up to expectations.[3] When it comes to randomness, Turing appears to foresee "fuzzy logic" machines: in other words, a machine where an approximation is sought as this can provide a quicker answer than anything that depends on 100% accuracy. Yet randomness is a human trait that depends very much on an individual's experience and background.

It is in 1952 that a machine that is recognised as the earliest form of artificial intelligence machine is presented by Marvin Minsky—the Stochastic Neural Analog Reinforcement Computer (*SNARC*). Following the lead of McCulloch and Pitts, who developed conceptual models of neuronal cells and the neural networks, Minsky attempted to recreate such a neural network using artificial (that is—electric and electronic) means.[4] Minsky (1958) starts out in a similar way as we have seen in Turing (1950). While there are points of disagreement, he also highlights that a digital computer needs to "learn" (by experience). Crucially, Minsky makes clear that a key task for any such machine is *pattern recognition*— something which then could lead to his proposed *semantic machine*.

This, admittedly, is an extremely concise history: details are easily found in other sources. It is against this background that the models discussed below—the focus of this book—have been developed.

2.2   M. Ross Quillian and the Language-Learning Machine

Given that current developments only really span comparatively few decades, it becomes very clear that access to powerful computing tools has made an impact on all sciences related to the human language. Today, it is hard to imagine that it was a tedious, complicated and time-con-suming process to assemble material for even just a small project in the 1960s. Computers that were given commands with the use of punch cards were the size of large rooms then. Still, machines filling halls the size of football fields had still less computing power than the average smartphone of 2018. And yet: though the methods could be seen as crude, and the working memories small by today's standards, a new era had started. Whereas early collections of words in context and intuitions about language use could be seen as valiant achievements of a lifetime; it was the availability of vast amounts of data, the computational process-ing power and ever-more sophisticated algorithms which would give a more grounded, far deeper and far better understanding of the structures found in languages and, likewise, create digital applications to process language.

M. Ross Quillian had received an MA in communications and then went on to do his PhD in Psychology. This, however, reveals little about the research scientist (for a defence consultant) who tried to create a computer program that simulates human natural language performance.[5] A closer look provides clear pointers that it was Quillian (1961, 1962, 1966, 1967, 1969; Collins and Quillian 1969) who provided the initial work in three key areas discussed here, namely *the semantic web*, *spread-ing activation* and *priming*. It appears that all the seminal works that past and current researches are based on go back, in one way or another, to this early research.

M. Ross Quillian described, as a broad outline, how to construct an understanding machine (1962)—and this was then expanded and more detailed when he presented the idea of a *Teachable Language Comprehender* (TLC 1969) a couple of years after getting his PhD on the subject of the *semantic memory*. Introducing the TLC, Quillian refers to language translation. There, he describes that one cannot imagine that a human translator would "translate directly". This means that no one would seriously think that every word in Language 1 has a direct equiv-alent in Language 2 or that word order can remain unchanged. Quillian concluded that a good mechanical translator can therefore not be expected to provide such a form of one-to-one translation either (1962: 17). In providing the theoretical blueprint for such a mechanical transla-tor, he tries to simulate how the human mind learns language.[6]

The result, presented in 1969, is a nifty little machine that is both trained on and self-learning through the source material provided as input. In a way, Quillian's example reminds the reader how a child would learn—which is no surprise, given his background training in psychology. According to Quillian, if the TLC is fed a set of texts with a similar topic (say: children's fiction or newspaper editorials), then the machine will be able to pick out not just the repeated words but also how and where these words are recurring, and whether they create a pattern that can be seen as phrasal or whether they use coherency markers that—thesaurus like—give the reader the notion of alternative ways to name the same (or strongly similar) issue. Quillian proposes a set of (only) twenty such texts. This must have sounded ambitious in the 1960s (one must also note that he looks at shorter texts, not, for example, full-sized novels). In the first quarter of the twenty-first century, we have seen that an almost unlimited amount of texts are computable: the big issue today is to find suitable material, clean it, boilerplate it and make it machine readable.[7]

Figure 2.1 is a random example to highlight how a machine can self-learn by creating a semantic web based on the textual material given as input. This is only a short excerpt—less than 200 words—yet it reveals semantic and structural qualities of the English language. If this looks confusing, it is half-intentional: the aim is to highlight points a *digital reader* who uses English science writing as training material would pick up (and this is not exhaustive). What follows are therefore just a few flashpoints to notice: The text presents near synonymy: lightning (line 2)

```
1   Some of the phenomena of electricity are manifested upon so large a scale
2   as to be thrust upon the attention of everybody. Thus lightning, which
3   accompanies so many showers in warm weather in almost every latitude, has
4   always excited in some individuals a superstitious awe, as being an
5   exhibition of supernatural agency; and probably every one feels more or
6   less dread of it during a thunder-shower, and this for the reason that it
7   affects so many of the senses at the same time. The flash may be blinding
8   to the eyes if near to us; the thunder may be deafening to the ears, and
9   so powerful as to shake the foundations of the hills, and make the ground
10  upon which we stand to sensibly move: these with the remembered
    destructive
11  effects that have been witnessed, of buildings demolished and large trees
12  torn to splinters in an instant, are quite sufficient to raise a feeling
13  of dread in the strongest mind. In the polar regions, both north and south,
14  where thunder-storms are less frequent, the atmospheric electricity
    assumes
15  the form called the aurora borealis, or the aurora australis, according
    as
16  it is seen north or south of the equator.[a]
```

[a](These lines are the opening paragraph of A. E. Dolbears 1877 book The Telephone: An Account of the Phenomena of Electricity, Magnetism, and Sound, as Involved in Its Action. With directions for making a speaking telephone)

Fig. 2.1 What a machine can learn from a short piece of text

is next referred to as flash (7). Lightning goes together with thunder. Thunder, furthermore, is closely connected to a particular kind of weather, namely showers (3), thunder shower (6), thunder (8) and thunderstorms (14). In fact, all of these seem to be linked to "warm weather" and "electricity". Moreover, there are a number of physical real-world concepts shown here: first, reference to the planet, which is split into segments: *latitude* (line 3), *polar regions* (13), *north and south* (13, 16) and *equator* (16). A reader would also take note that *north* is presented before *south*. Second, the link between *superstition* (line 4) and *supernatural agency* (5) which may induce feelings of "dread" (6). Moreover, there is *blinding* which connects to *eyes* and *deafening* noises which can affect *ears* (7–8). As a last point, it must be noted that this also provides a template for grammatical patterns and structures. In the last example, *to the* is repeated: *to* being here (like in *near to*, line 8) in the word category *preposition*. Nevertheless, there are also another use of *to*—like in line (2), "to be thrust" or line (12) "to raise", which is the *to-Infinitive*. This is also the case for the usage pattern of *of*, which repeatedly appears as *of the*; the meaning of *so*, which appears as a booster, in particular for uncountable quantities and so on. This is simply a brief, concise demonstration—yet all of this would assist in creating a semantic web.

Thus, Quillian describes that the TLC will be able to comprehend a text given to it, because the comprehender will have learned from its training input:

> What the reader must have, then, as he reads the text (…), is an extremely versatile ability to recognize the appropriate chunk of memory information from among literally thousands of others he may since have learned about 'Presidents,' about 'fruit trees,' and about 'fathers'. […] we assume that there is a common core process that underlies the reading of all text – newspapers, children's fiction, or whatever – and it is this core process that TLC attempts to model.[8] (1969: 461)

Here, we can see how Quillian proposes to leave the machine to figure out words in contexts. Later (1969: 464), he outlines how the input for the Teachable Language Comprehender could consist of a small batch—twenty different children's books dealing with firemen—to let the machine understand the basics about firefighters. This, for him, would be a digital way of copying the comprehension apparatus that humans develop as they learn a language:

> Natural language text communicates by causing a reader to recall mental concepts that he already has. It refers him to such already known concepts either with isolated words or with short phrases, and then specifies or implies particular relations between these. (1969: 474)

In other words, in natural language the mind is set to connect concepts on hearing or reading words and short phrases.

In fact, Quillian points out that as the comprehender searches his or her memory, it is "looking for properties which can be considered related to that text" (1969: 474)—and therefore, the comprehender in its digital incarnation should mirror what a human communicator does.

Quillian reckons that his TLC is fully teachable—not by working on big structures but by learning piece by piece. The structure would thereby develop through what is feasible and what is not. Once we substitute *Speaker / Writer* for the term *Machine*, it becomes clear that Quillian (1969: 475) gives a good grounding for the research into the *semantic* web to come. Crucially, he claims that the most distinctive and superior features of his theory are "its explicitness and detail and its reliance on 'knowledge of the world'".

2.3   QUILLIAN, COLLINS AND LOFTUS: THE *SEMANTIC WEB* AND FACILITATING ACCESS TO THE *SEMANTIC MEMORY*

In the early 1960s, a thought concept of an "understanding machine" is presented by Ross Quillian (1962). Quillian himself admits that it may take huge efforts to build such an information retrieval machine: "it is clear that actually building such a memory involves a gigantic amount of work, and very tedious and dirty work" (ibid.: 29). Still, at the end will be a machine possessing a semantic *memory*. He was right in a way—he just did not spell out that "gigantic amount of work" meant the expenditure of a huge amount of time, revision of original models and going down a number of blind alleys. Amongst other things, the 1962 text describes how "blocks of texts"—that is, the corpus of source material—are being moved to positions of quicker or slower retrieval. It is open to speculation whether this reflects Quillian's conceptual thinking. Could it be that he wanted to replicate the idea of human memory—things which are frequently retrieved are easily accessible, while items that are rarely called for seem to be lodged in deeper recesses of the human memory? Or, alternatively, did he think along the lines of the typical model of a solid-state retrieval system then available: a library. In a library, frequently borrowed ("retrieved") books are found in the open, accessible areas of the building. Material rarely consulted is, however, located in storage. Storage, furthermore, that is divided into areas with easy access (books which are located on-site), or where retrieval will take longer (located off-site). Quillian, in 1962, sees it as a "complex problem to decide which block of information [to be put] at what depth" (ibid.: 28). The issue does, however, appear outdated in the twenty-first century, where access to any material already digitized is not determined by the computing facilities available but, more likely, are based on the subscriptions or other arrangements made to give access to such material. Despite such obvious limitations, Quillian had, in his *Revised Design for an Understanding Machine*, described the fundamental ability of a semantic memory computer, namely to "provide different kinds of information for resolving polysemies"—a capability that is based on a set of natural language material (1962: 28).[9] One key issue is that any kind resolution of a polysemantic ambiguity ultimately consists of exploiting clues in the words, sentences or paragraphs of text that surround that word. Such clues would ascertain that alternative meanings are far less likely; consequently, only one of its meanings is found to be appropriate for that particular context. Furthermore, the location and arrangement in which we find these markers is itself a clue, or rather a set of clues, and these may be called *syntactic clues* (cf. Quillian 1962: 17).

The problem of polysemy can be demonstrated in an ambiguous sentence like "He reached the bank" but not in "He got a loan from the bank". In the latter, the clues are sufficient, as Quillian explains:

> Thus, in our example, a reference to money is one such semantic clue, and one which, should it appear in the sentence, could be exploited no matter what word it occurred in, whether one of those on our list or not. [...] Learning to understand a language would consist of learning which readings on which scales should be activated in response to each word of that language. (1962: 18)

Quillian actively spurns transformational linguistics.[10] This becomes clear when he compares his approach to "mechanical translation" to the attempts by others to circumvent the problematic issue of managing "presentations of meaning" (1962: 18). He finds that simply "using grammatical features and their locations, or else (...) in established idiomatic phrases to resolve polysemantic ambiguities" is too simple and falls short of producing satisfactory results. Quillian is clear sighted enough to point out that this would not give a machine all the available clues:

> That human beings do not so limit themselves, but also utilize semantic clues extensively, would appear obvious from the fact that people are able to understand language that is full of grammatical and syntactical errors.[11] (1962: 18)

Optimistically, Quillian describes that such an understanding machine would have repercussions beyond the field of "fully automatic, high quality translation":

> For information retrieval, and for social science, the implications of having a computer program able to reproduce the essentials of human understanding of language would seem to be of no small importance. (1962: 29)

This resembles Quillian's description of a machine reader that has built up a semantic web in its memory:

> This memory is a 'semantic network' representing factual assertions about the world.
> The program also creates copies of the parts of its memory which have been found to relate to the new text, adapting and combining these copies to represent the meaning of the new text. By this means, the meaning of all text the program successfully comprehends is encoded into the same format as that of the memory. In this form it can be added into the memory. (1969: 459)

With this, Quillian also describes, in a slightly different fashion, the aims of this book: understanding how one particular technology does not only have practical applications (which can result in huge, digital computing-led productivity gains)—there is also the benefit gained as the computational construct presents a model of how to understand both language and characteristics of human society, in particular the nature of human discourses.

In 1966, Quillian was working on a research project for the *US Airforce Research Laboratories* which resulted in his doctoral thesis on *semantic memory*. Quillian highlights that it is "precisely because of a growing interdependence between ... linguistic theory and psychological performance models" (1966: 165) that further research into the nature of language processing must be undertaken. In describing his model, he starts off by making a number of crucial distinctions. For one, he points out that the language users employ *recognition memory* as opposed to *recall memory*. He gives a very clear example of how to differentiate these—and makes the importance of such a difference instantly clear. To illustrate, he points out that "if a reader is told that the word 'the' can mean 'her' [the reader] may not immediately *recall*[12] how this can be so". In order to make clear how this semantic meaning of "the" comes about, an example is given. One has to picture an occasion where the reader comes across the following statement: "I took my wife by the hand" (Quillian 1966: 4). Having *recall* of possible meaning of "the" would most possibly mean that a reader defines this as a grammatical word, one that is used as a determiner but with little or no information content. However, as a reader it will be recognised that the "the" in "I took my wife by the hand" could be replaced by the personal pronoun "her": "I took my wife by her hand". "Her", like "the", can be classed as determiners, yet only the process of recognition will ensure that a reader sees the latter as back referential to the wife. Going beyond that, Quillian highlights that, to that date, little research into the long-term memory of language users has been undertaken. He sets his concept of language processing into a decisive contrast to the model then proposed by the likes of Chomsky and Lakoff. The model Quillian describes looks strangely familiar and contemporary: similar to the model that Minsky used, Quillian talks of *nodes* which are interconnected by *associative links*.[13] In his papers, Quillian describes how every *node* (word) is in receipt of single *tag* and this tag creates a link once reference to another node becomes active. The nodes are single words which can directly refer to the meaning: this would indicate a system that provides equivalence, similar to a dictionary:

This seems, oddly enough, like the recall system that would be called into question the moment recognition is required. A table in a sentence like "these results are summarised in Table 5" is clearly a different entity than the one shown in Fig. 2.2. In fact, the notion of words being directly associated with a meaning had to be withdrawn as a result of later experiments Quillian and his colleagues undertook. The part of his model that stood the test of time appears to be the association of an indirect kind, namely that a word's meaning can be deducted from a

Fig. 2.2 "Directly associated *table*"—where a word is equivalent to a single entity

combination of other word meanings—words that are found linked to the original node. In Quillian's words, "[t]he particular configuration of these word concepts is crucial; it both modifies the meanings of the individual word concepts that make up its parts and creates a new *gestalt* with them, which represents the meaning of the word being defined" (Quillian 1966: 14).

This quote refers to three extremely important facts when it comes to disambiguating the meaning—uncovering the semantic value—of a node (word). Firstly, the strength of the *associative link* is seen as relevant. This is the "particular configuration". Secondly, a node has not got a direct, dictionary-like meaning: meaning is created through the meanings of the other words found in the associative link. Thirdly, these meanings are created anew ("given *gestalt*") with each different set of *associative links*. This hints at a potentially enormous amount of flexibility. Consequently, both the opportunities that the meanings associated with one word fluctuate, depending on the immediate context it is used in. It does, furthermore, leave considerable room for creativity. A simple example can demonstrate how this works:

Looking at the *associative links*[14] of "house", "of" and "master", it can be seen that these are all words that link to the node "mistress" in nineteenth-century fiction. By comparison, the words "his" and "young" are words that link to the node "mistress" in twentieth-century fiction. This gives us a hint that the phrase "master and mistress of the house" could still be found in use during the twentieth century. However, they were predominantly used in the 1800s, when "mistress" was somebody who was in charge of a household (often in conjunction with the "master"). One century on, and a "mistress" refers, more often than not, to a man's non-spouse, often younger. Notably, these *associative links* are not grounded in grammatical structures. Quillian (1966: 164) goes even further and concludes that the notion of a semantic memory has a number of implications, amongst them the following:

- dichotomous judgements of semantic well-formedness vs. anomaly are not essential or inherent to language performance
- sentence understanding should be treated as simply a problem of extracting a cognitive representation of a text's message
- until some theoretical notion of cognitive representation is incorporated into linguistic conceptions, they are unlikely to provide either powerful language-processing programs or psychologically relevant theories.

These, in short, can be seen as cornerstones of a descriptivist-empirical approach to (any) language. In fact, the first of these points seems to indicate that "well-formed" and "anomalous" utterances are standing side by side with and being typical of language as we find it. Furthermore, rather than focusing on a single word, understanding should focus on the outcome—and this is relevant regardless of the length of the text. The final point can, of course, be seen as self-serving: Quillian does, after all, present his theory here, and he is a cognitive scientist. The point to be made is, however, that Quillian is, indeed, referred to in most of the literature dealing with the origins of the semantic web—which is based on this, his early theoretical work.

Moving on from the theory, Collins and Quillian (1969, 1970, 1971, 1972a, 1972b) conducted a series of experiments. The research involved measuring the reaction times of volunteers to find out that "true sentences" (tennis is a game) have a shorter reaction time than "false sentences"[15] (football is a lottery). The seminal text here is Collins and Quillian's (1969) *Retrieval from the Semantic Memory*. This became the foundation for experiments by psycholinguists, including Loftus (1973), Posner and Snyder (1975), Collins and Loftus (1975), and as well as Ashcraft (1976). Significantly, it led to the seminal paper by Meyer and Schvaneveldt, *Facilitation in Recognizing Pairs of Words: Evidence of a Dependence Between Retrieval Operations* (1971). Meyer and Schvaneveldt's paper links an insight derived from psycholinguistic experimental evidence with the original theory. Meyer and Schvaneveldt refine and expand the scope of the 1969 experiment undertaken by Collins and Quillian. In the 1971 version, candidates are tasked to link each of a set of English words to either (a) unassociated words or (b) related words. The pair measured the *reaction times* (RTs) in order to detect any differences:

> We showed that such decisions are faster when one word (e.g., 'nurse') is preceded by another semantically related word (e.g., 'doctor'). [than linked with a unassociated word, e.g. *bread*]
> [Positive] responses averaged 85 ± 19 msec. faster for pairs of associated words than for pairs of unassociated words. (1971: 20)

The response time for *semantically related words*, then, was shown to be decisively quicker than the ones for *unassociated words*, indicating that the listener/reader makes a subconscious mental connection between these two *nodes*. Meyer and Schvaneveldt point out that their results "suggest that degree of association is a powerful factor affecting lexical decisions [the choice of word(s) made by the subject in the experiment] in the [...] task" (1971: 229). It must be noted, furthermore, that the differences in the response times were found to be significant. Meyer and Schvaneveldt go on to claim that this is a mental process that does not only reside in the short-term memory. They refer to McCormick (1959) who had already highlighted that the human long-term memory does not function like the *random access memory* (RAM) of current computers.

The idea of a hierarchical representation of semantic concepts in the mind, as described in Quillian (1966), is found to be less relevant in Loftus and Loftus (1974) and Collins and Loftus (1975). What experiments did show, however, is that related semantic fields can appear to show shorter *association links*. This was shown in the experiments by David Meyer (1973) who describes his, Collins and Quillian's earlier experiments. The notion described by Quillian in 1962—with close and distant storage facilities—had to be revised. Memory structure is said to "var[y] directly with their closeness of meaning, and that the duration of successive retrieval operations increases with the 'semantic distance' between words" (Meyer 1973: 124). Meyer's research shows that, even when the "semantic distance" is based on intuitive choices, faster reaction times can be observed. This does not necessarily mean that a brain works with word fields as a superordinate facility. What happens instead is that the broad category (in other words, the word field) appears to give the mind easier facilitation to access the expected word. Meyer therefore refers back to work he was involved in two years earlier where he already referred to the *proximity of associated words*—one word acts as prime and the mind is set to expect a limited set of options to follow.

2.4   The Issue of Spreading Activation

It must be noted that Quillian himself, in his early works, did not speak of *spreading activation* at all. In Quillian (1962), the reference is to *neural activation,* and in Quillian (1966), he speaks of *activation spheres* and the *activation process*. In fact, the term *spreading activation*, closely linked to *priming* (Sect. 2.5), has been introduced by Collins and Loftus in 1975, namely with their paper *A Spreading-Activation Theory of Semantic Processing*. According to the authors, Quillian first described the concept in 1965, in an unpublished version of the Quillian (1967) paper. Looking back, Allan Collins provided some further information recently. "... the first I remember our using the term was in experiments where we had a sentence semantically prime a subsequent sentence. My memory is I borrowed the term from some of the psycholinguistic work at the time which was the 1970s."[16] In fact, the term *priming* seems to appear for the first time in Collins and Quillian (1971). The paper is, in effect, a further development from his PhD. It develops a model for a psychological theory which reaches the point where it merges with *information processing theory*. The principle is best summed up by Collins and Loftus:

> Some years ago, Quillian (1962, 1967) proposed a *spreading-activation theory of human semantic processing* that he tried to implement in computer simulations of memory search (Quillian 1966) and comprehension (Quillian 1969). ... The effects of preparation (or priming) in semantic memory were also explained in terms of spreading activation from the node of the primed concept. Rather than a theory to explain data, it was a theory designed to show how to build human semantic structure and processing into a computer. (Collins and Loftus 1975: 407; author's highlights)

The crucial point here is that Quillian provides a concept that can then be developed further—either in the direction of looking at the use of a long-term memory of a human being or as a theory to develop a computer program which is able to retrieve information based on a semantic memory principle. We have seen in Sect. 2.3 that a different combination of nodes can lead to different reaction times, i.e. (R_1)*bird*-(R_2)*wings* has a shorter reaction time than $(R_1)bird$-$mouth(R_3)$. This reflects the strength of accessibility from one node (here: *bird*) to another. There is more of an activation spread between (R_1) and (R_2), the reason being a relatively high frequency of a combination of the two. This does not necessarily mean that R_1 has to be directly following R_2—the two as direct neighbours as in *bird wings*. It is sufficient to have them in proximity: *wings* of a *bird*, the *bird* spread its *wings*, etc. As Collins and Loftus describe it, "the amount the first concept primes the second concept determines the reaction time" (ibid.: 417).

According to Ashcraft, the processes of *spreading activation* and *priming* are linked—they are the phenomena that enable access to the semantic *information*:

> Collins and Quillian proposed that the *spread of activation* or *priming* represents the basic mechanism of accessing semantic information. *Activation spreads* down the relational paths ... resulting in greater *priming* of properties which are highly related (dominant) to the concept. (Ashcraft 1976: 491; author's highlights)

One might think of a coin where *priming* is found on one side, and *spreading activation* on the other, yet that would be wrong. According to Yorick Wilks,[17] "*spreading activation* is a procedural theory over networks and it could implement a whole range of phenomena and has done". The person who dealt with it most directly, Allan Collins, describes the two concepts thus:

> *Activation spreads* from concepts that are triggered in Ross [Quillian's] view. *Priming* can be viewed as potentiation of a node that has been reached previously by spreading activation. Hence the concept triggers more easily or faster because it is potentiated, when presented with a later statement or question. My original study with Ross related to spreading activation, whereas later experiments involved priming when I studied how the processing of previous questions affected the processing of later questions.[18] (author's highlights)

This might be explained with the help of Fig. 2.3. Typically, of course, the spread would be a lot wider.

In the example, BIRD acts as a trigger and spreads to activate several nodes. As a consequence, the words *black*, *little*, *big* and *eye* are primed. As will be shown below, this *process of priming* needs a further element: *repeat exposure*. Therefore, for example, fans of *Sesame Street* will have

Fig. 2.3 Activation
spreads from the trigger
BIRD to several nodes

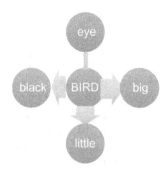

heard (and seen) BIG BIRD quite often; it can also be purely descriptive—like little bird or black bird, something a typical British speaker would have heard people say often.[19] Therefore, relatively strong links can be found between the trigger and the node. Yet, when we look at BIRD in connection with *eye*, the link is a lot weaker; for one thing, the possessive marker '*s*' is missing. And, while the reader or listener might see or hear instances of "bird eye", there is no direct priming. Instances of the possessive marker would enable the strong link of BIRDS with "eye", "nest", etc.

2.5   QUILLIAN AND THE PSYCHOLOGICAL CONCEPT OF PRIMING[20]

As we have seen above, early research into computational intelligence tried to replicate how thought processes function in neural networks. Intriguingly, it was the attempt to create a machine to understand language that led to a clearer understanding of a neural process: namely, how information is fixed in and accessed from memory. It is what psychology refers to as *priming*. The *Sage Handbook of Social Psychology* provides the following characterisation of priming. It describes the main tenets of the theory in the context of psychology and is therefore quoted here at length:

The activation of stored knowledge through experiences in the immediate context can make prime-relevant information more accessible in memory, and such recent construct activation can influence inferences, evaluations, and decisions on subsequent tasks. A second factor that influences the accessibility of information in memory is the frequency with which a construct has been primed. (Sherman et al. 2003: 55)

As far as priming is concerned, this description neatly sums it up. Sherman and colleagues describe how the human brain has access to memories in a structured form, with information being accessed more easily when it can be linked to other landmarks or to otherwise readily accessible information. Crucially, these links multiply and firm up the more often a person is exposed to the same or a very similar pattern or information bundle.

Figure 2.4 gives a very simple demonstration. The sentence (1) is a classic example in English language teaching—this leads the author to assume that the reader has come across this particular sentence (at least once) before. Line one has six words: six *tokens* and five *types* (as "the" occurs twice). The shapes indicate different grammatical categories. Sentence (1) also has three minimal pairs: C*AT*, S*AT* and M*AT*, as has been highlighted. In (2), CAT is the prime, and it activates the other

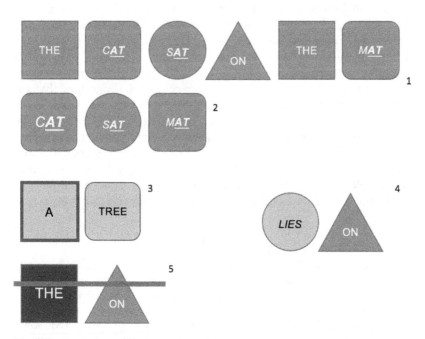

Fig. 2.4 Activation spreading and priming

lexical words, which also happen to be the other words of the set of minimal pairs with AT. In (3), the prime is the word category (article). In this case, it does not matter that the prime and the activated word are not lexical; the prime simply activates a structure: *article* is followed by *noun*. Something similar happens in (4) where the structural prime *verb* is followed by a preposition. Finally, example number (5) describes a dispreferred pattern: the word *the* does not prime to activate the word *on*; similarly, an article does not act as a prime to be followed by a preposition. This is, of course, a highly simplified model, and the process of *firming up* through repeat exposure is not demonstrated here—apart from one tiny yet crucial form of repetition: the recurrent sound in the minimal pairs, that is the sound /æt/.[21]

Priming is seen, overall, less of a linguistic concept and much more of a psychological one, yet the range of applications are many—one simply has to point back to Minsky's work in the 1950s where he aimed at rebuilding neural networks. Sherman et al. rightly point to the research articles published by Quillian between 1961 and 1969. According to Collins and Loftus, it was Ross Quillian, who they describe as a "cognitive scientist",[22] who first used the term: "Quillian's theory of *semantic memory* search and semantic preparation, or *priming*" (1975: 409; author's highlights). Looking at the number of research publications (including a large number not mentioned here—in particular those undertaken by Elizabeth Loftus and her colleagues), one sees that the 1970s turned out to be extremely fruitful period for laboratory-based experiments. These presented an ever-increasing body of evidence supporting the validity of the theory[23] as the two papers by James H. Neely (1976, 1977)[24] show. In fact, the title—*Semantic Priming and Retrieval from Lexical Memory*[25]—makes clear how Neely maps the process of how the neurological network has been "programed" (that is, primed) to understand a word based on the item presented prior to this word.

NOTES

1. See Russell and Norvig (1995) and Wegner and Goldin (2003) for details.
2. In fact, Turing seems to be politely fair. On page 435, he says that "we do not wish to penalise the machine for its inability to shine in beauty competitions, nor to penalise a mam for losing a race against an aeroplane".
3. In spring 2016, Microsoft presented a "chatbot" called TAY which "learned" off Twitter feeds. Apparently, less than 24 hours after its

launch, the "feeders" had turned TAY into a bot spouting racist rubbish. On a more serious note, a lot of researchers have pointed out that machines seem to have been fed with material echoing the programers' (unconscious) prejudices, which means that job applications are rated highest when they mirror the qualifications of the recruiting board; faces of white participants are being recognised by their features, whereas dark-skinned people at times have been identified as animals, etc.

4. See Kelemen (2007) for details.
5. These details are taken from the author's blurb in *Behavioural Sciences* 12 (1967).
6. "The program's strategy is presented as a general theory of language comprehension", Quillian (1969).
7. This means material that is not seen in breach of copyright or privacy rules. While written texts are relatively easy to obtain, spoken material relies on labour-intensive transcription. Texts obtained must be made machine-readable but headers and legal disclaimers are often cut out. Lastly, boiler-plating means to find and delete duplicate texts.
8. Quillian refers to *The Fable of George Washington and the Cherry Tree*. Washington is here described as a young boy who felled his father's cherry tree. This particular example appears to fit into the category of "common knowledge" in the USA. Readers in Britain, however, (me included) could not really relate to this story. Therefore, the example might be unsuitable. In this context, it does highlight a crucial characteristic that Quillian unknowingly brought to the fore: inbuilt bias. We are confronted, as a result, with AI applications that cannot recognise female voices (as the tool had been designed by and trained with only male voices, which tend to have a deeper timbre). There are quite a number of such cases, all highlighted widely in press articles found in 2016 and 2017. These highlight a crucial blind spot in the current stage of development.
9. Apparently, Marvin Minsky referred to words that carry a variety of semantic meanings as "suitcase words"—possibly because of the link of "carry" and "collect different, not necessarily related entities in one container".
10. "The relation between TLC, a semantic performance model, and the syntactic 'competence' models of transformational linguistics (Chomsky 1965) is not clear. The efforts that have been made so far to attach 'semantics' to transformational models seem, to this writer at least, to have achieved little success" (Quillian 1969).
11. Meyer and Schvaneveldt (1976) suggest that Quillian is proved right in an experiment where words are made harder to read.
12. Author's highlights.

13. Like in corpus linguistics, Quillian refers to any given English word as "the node" unlike corpus linguistics, he does not then move from the node-word to n-grams (collocations) but speaks of *associative links*.
14. This particular experiment has been conducted by looking at the collocates of these words in corpora of nineteenth- and twentieth-century fiction. That the word *mistress* changes its meaning over time is an example originally used by Michael Hoey during his Discourse Studies undergraduate seminars at The University of Liverpool.
15. "True" and "false" sentences are the terminology used by Collins and Quillian.
16. Personal communication, e-mail, April 2018.
17. Personal communication, e-mail, October 2017.
18. Personal communication, e-mail, October 2017.
19. The example given here is based on the closest collocates of BIRD/ BIRD'S in casual spoken British English corpora. "Blackbird", being a single entity, is not considered here.
20. Some parts of Chapters 2 and 3 will have first been published in Pace-Sigge (2013).
21. Stefan Gries points out that sound-similarity seems to be an inherent feature of a number of (semi-) idiomatic phrases in the English language. See his article "Phonological Similarity in Multi-word Units" (2011).
22. In fact, Quillian is also referred to as a *computer scientist* and a *social scientist*. I guess this just highlights how the subject of cognitive science is important to all manners of applications.
23. Neely in Neely et al. (1991) describes how Posner and Snyder's work was his main influence and how they were influenced by Meyer and Schvaneveldt. All four appear in the bibliography of Neely (1977).
24. Which Michael Hoey (2005) refers to on p. 8 of *Lexical Priming*.
25. Neely published what amounts to almost the same paper with different subtitles in two different publications in two consecutive years.

REFERENCES

Ashcraft, Mark H. 1976. Priming and Property Dominance Effects in Semantic Memory. *Memory and Cognition* 4 (5): 490–500.
Chomsky, N. (1965). *Aspects of the Theory of Syntax*. Cambridge, Massachusetts: The MIT Press.
Collins, Allan M., and M. Ross Quillian. 1969. Retrieval Time from Semantic Memory. *Journal of Verbal Learning and Verbal Behaviour* 8 (2): 240–248.
Collins, Allan M., and M. Ross Quillian. 1970. Facilitating Retrieval from Semantic Memory: The Effect of Repeating Part of an Inference. *Acta Psychologica* 33: 304–314.

Collins, Allan M., and M. Ross Quillian. 1971. Information Processess in Models and Computer Aids for Human Performance. Final Report, Section 4, task 4: Studies of Human Memory and Language Processing. APRA Order No. 890, Amendment No. 5. Bolt Beranek and Newman Inc.

Collins, Allan M., and M. Ross Quillian. 1972a. Experiments on Semantic Memory and Language Comprehension. In *Cognition in Learning and Memory*, ed. L.W. Gregg. New York: Wiley.

Collins, Allan M., and M. Ross Quillian. 1972b. How to Make a Language User. In *Organisation of Memory*, ed. E. Tulving and W. Donaldson, 319–322. New York: Academic Press.

Collins, Allan M., and Elizabeth F. Loftus. 1975. A Spreading-Activation Theory of Semantic Processing. *Psychological Review* 82 (6): 407–428.

Gries, Stefan. 2011. Phonological Similarity in Multi-word Units. *Cognitive Linguistics* 22 (3): 491–510.

Hoey, Michael. 2005. *Lexical Priming: A New Theory of Words and Language*. London: Routledge.

Kelemen, Jozef. 2007. From Artificial Neural Networks to Emotion Machines with Marvin Minsky. *Acta Polytechnica Hungarica* 4 (4): 5–16.

Loftus, Elizabeth F. 1973. Activation of Semantic Memory. *American Journal of Psychology* 86 (2): 331–337.

Loftus, G.R., and E.F. Loftus. 1974. The Influence of One Memory Retrieval on a Subsequent Memory Retrieval. *Memory and Cognition* 2: 467–471.

McCormick, E. M. 1959. *Digital Computer Primer*. New York: McGraw-Hill.

McCulloch, Warren S., and Walter Pitts. 1943. A Logical Calculus of the Ideas Immanent in Nervous Activity. *The Bulletin of Mathematical Biophysics* 5 (4): 115–133.

Meyer, David E. 1973. Correlated Operations in Searching Stored Semantic Categories. *Journal of Experimental Psychology* 99 (1): 124–133.

Meyer, David E., and Roger W. Schvaneveldt. 1971. Facilitation in Recognizing Pairs of Words: Evidence of a Dependence Between Retrieval Operations. *Journal of Experimental Psychology* 90 (2): 227–234.

Meyer, David E., and Roger W. Schvaneveldt. 1976. Meaning, Memory Structure and Mental Processes. *Science* 192 (4234) (April 2): 27–33.

Minsky, Marvin L. 1952. A Neural-Analogue Calculator Based Upon a Probability Model of Reinforcement. *Harvard University Psychological Laboratories*, Cambridge, MA.

Minsky, Marvin L. 1958. Some Methods of Artificial Intelligence and Heuristic Programming. In *Proceedings of the Symposium on the Mechanization of Thought Processes*, Teddington.

Neely, James H. 1976. Semantic Priming and Retrieval from Lexical Memory: Evidence for Facilitatory and Inhibitory Processes. *Memory and Cognition* 4 (5): 648–654.

Neely, James H. 1977. Semantic Priming and Retrieval from Lexical Memory: Roles of Inhibitionless Spreading Activation and Limited-Capacity Attention. *Journal of Experimental Psychology: General* 106 (3): 226–254.

Neely, J. H. 1991. Semantic Priming Effects in Visual Word Recognition: A Selective Review of Current Findings and Theories. In *Basic processes in reading: Visual word recognition*, eds. D. Besner & G. Humphreys, 264–336. Hillsdale, NJ: Erlbaum.

Pace-Sigge, Michael. 2013. *Lexical Priming in Spoken English Usage*. Basingstoke: Palgrave Macmillan.

Posner, Michael L., and Charles Richard R. Snyder. 1975. Facilitation and Inhibition in the Processing of Signals. In *Attention and Performance V*, ed. P.M.A. Rabbitt and S. Domi, 669–681. New York: Academic Press.

Quillian, M. Ross 1961. The Elements of Human Meaning: A Design for and Understanding Machine. *Communications of the ACM* 4 (9) (September): 406.

Quillian, M. Ross. 1962. A Revised Design for an Understanding Machine. *Mechanical Translation* 7: 17–29.

Quillian, M. Ross. 1966. *Semantic Memory*. Unpublished Doctoral Dissertation, Carnegie Institute of Technology (Reprinted in Part in M. Minsky (ed.), *Semantic Information Processing*. Cambridge: MIT Press, 1968).

Quillian, M. Ross. 1967. Word Concepts: A Theory and Simulation of Some Basic Semantic Capabilities. *Behavioral Science* 12: 410–430.

Quillian, M. Ross. 1969. The Teachable Language Comprehender: A Simulation Program and Theory of Language. *Computational Linguistics* 12 (8) (August): 459–476.

Russell, Stuart and Peter Norvig. 1995. *Artificial Intelligence: A Modern Approach*, 1st edn, Prentice-Hall, NJ.: Englewood Cliffs.

Sherman, Steven J., Matthew T. Crawford, David L. Hamilton, and Leonel Garcia-Marques. 2003. Social Inference and Social Memory: The Interplay Between Systems. In *The SAGE Handbook of Social Psychology*, ed. Michael Hogg and Joel Cooper, 45–67. London: Sage.

Turing, Alan M. 1937a. On Computable Numbers, with an Application to the Enscheidungsproblem. *Proceedings of the London Mathematical Society* 2 (42): 230–265.

Turing, Alan M. 1937b. Computability and λ-Definability. *The Journal of Symbolic Logic* 2 (4): 153–163.

Turing, Alan M. 1950. Computing Machinery and Intelligence. *Mind, New Series* 59 (236): 433–460.

Wegner, Peter, and Dina Goldin. 2003. Computation Beyond Turing Machines. *Communications of the ACM* 46 (4): 100–102.

Wittgenstein, Ludwig. [1949] 1953. *Philosophical Investigations*. Oxford: Basil Blackwell.

CHAPTER 3

Where Corpus Linguistics and Artificial Intelligence (AI) Meet

Abstract This chapter will provide a platform to showcase the more recent developments that have grown out of the early laid groundwork. The latest theories in the field of linguistics will be presented, based on empirical data taken from naturally occurring language. In particular, the lexical priming theory will be introduced as a way to explain structures of language that corpus linguists have uncovered. Furthermore, the chapter will discuss the development of increasingly sophisticated algorithms that also deal with the use of language. Here, the focus will be on key achievements in the 1980s by IBM which created a solid foundation for applications that are now widely used in mobile and desktop devices—namely "assistants" like Amazon's *Echo*, Apple's *SIRI* or Google's (and Android's) *Google Go*.

Keywords Hoey · Quillian · Norvig · Lexical priming · LSTM
N-gram model · Digital translators

3.1 Introduction

This chapter describes how the ideas and concepts developed by Ross Quillian were taken up by psycholinguists, corpus linguists and Artificial Intelligence (AI) researchers in different ways in order to further their investigations. In Sect. 3.2, an introduction to and an overview of

© The Author(s) 2018   29
M. Pace-Sigge, *Spreading Activation,*
Lexical Priming and the Semantic Web,
https://doi.org/10.1007/978-3-319-90719-2_3

Michael Hoey's *lexical priming* theory, which tries to explain the language structures shown by corpus linguists, relates to Ross Quillian's early work on language models. This is then followed by showing how Quillian's theory, in particular the notion of *spreading activation* and *reinforcement learning* served as a basis for developing concepts of *machine learning* (ML). Sections 3.5 and 3.6 complete the chapter by describing the latest developing in mimicking neural networks and a number of applications are demonstrated here.

3.2   FROM QUILLIAN'S *PRIMING* TO HOEY'S *LEXICAL PRIMING*

We have seen in Chapter 2 how the concept of "priming" evolved out of Ross Quillian's seminal work. "Priming" together with "lexical" appears to be first brought into discussion by James H. Neely (1976), who provides the link between research undertaken in the 1960s and 1970s to Hoey's corpus linguistics-based theory of *lexical priming* (2005). He specifically references Neely, yet does not give any further details on the link between Neely's psycholinguistic experiments and Hoey's own interpretation.

Hoey (2005) notes that *lexical priming* does not simply mean connecting lexically and semantically related words. In fact, some primes (e.g. *very*) have little lexical content. That these still play an important role in semantic memory is pointed out by Quillian (1969). Meyer and Schvaneveldt highlight that it is not necessarily the "meaning" of a word that makes it act as a prime, and call for further investigation. The issue of priming and meaning shall be returned to later.

The idea of *lexical priming* can be traced back to the concept of *bonding* (Hoey 1991)—work which has provided a basic framework for the theory[1]:

> From childhood onwards, we effortlessly acquire a large vocabulary of items that, barring malapropisms, we use and recognize without trouble. Of these items, only a tiny proportion will have been defined for us; for only a few more will a dictionary have been consulted. The remainder we will have acquired without deliberate help. *Given that one of the most productive ways of defining is by placing a word in a characteristic context, it seems sensible to assume that as we acquire language (and indeed ever after), we build up meaning profiles using context.* That presupposes that we retain access to the contexts of words previously encountered, or else each new encounter with a word of whose meaning we were uncertain would be a fresh problem. (Hoey 1991: 155, author's highlights)

This should sound familiar to the reader, because it appears to be a direct echo of how Quillian describes his Teachable Language Comprehender (TLC)—see Sect. 2.2. There is the clear reference to a child's language acquisition and that meaning is deducted from context. In fact, Hoey goes one step further in saying that "we acquire language" this way—therefore, not just the semantics but also set patterns: the grammatical (and, indeed, phonetical) structures these words are found in. The result of this is an assembly of meaning profiles that language users have created by storing lexical items in their specific contexts. Hoey (1991) compares this kind of storage to the way texts are presented in corpus linguistics: that is, in concordance lines (see Fig. 3.1).

The item *encounter* has been chosen because it appears twice in the quote above. We can observe a strong preference for the verb form, *to encounter*, and there is also a noun form (*the/that encounter*). It is people (*him, her, man, Miss Kenton, Paula*, etc.) mostly but also wild animals (a tiger) or something more abstract (death) that are encountered. This example, based on novels by different writers, written in different years, demonstrates the idea of bonding and how Hoey sees relationships between words stored in writers' minds.

This would also explain how we try to explain words to a language learner ad hoc: "When we define a word to each other informally, we typically exemplify the word's uses" (Hoey 1991: 154). Hoey also describes that *bonding* is not the same as *collocation*: mostly, the bonds are not found in adjacent sentences (see Fig. 2.1 and its discussion above), while collocates are near (usually within the range of five words to the left or right) to the target word. Poignantly, Hoey back in 1991 (p. 149) describes that one would need a thorough, computational

with her after a few words with Mr Darling. The ENCOUNTER with him had left Maggie with an uneasy
Lachlan Cattanach was an unchancy man to ENCOUNTER. Not a few men lost teeth because they
Yet I must say, something about this small ENCOUNTER had put me in very good spirits; the simple
the occasion around that time I happened to ENCOUNTER her in the back corridor. The back corridor
As I hastened to go upstairs, I happened to ENCOUNTER Miss Kenton in the back corridor the scene,
although I am sure he never had the chance to ENCOUNTER a tiger beneath the dining table, when
less fussy. Paula certainly never seemed to ENCOUNTER such problems. She had a string of boyfriends
So, that woman is many English children's first ENCOUNTER with death, lying there, knees to chin
trouble with The Sex Pistols on TV. You miss the ENCOUNTER, but realize abruptly that you are a
warmth continues to grow with every subsequent ENCOUNTER, as though it were natural for human

Fig. 3.1 A selection of concordance lines of the word *encounter* (BNC Written-Fiction)

study in order to find sufficient evidence of bonding over long stretches of text. This particular issue is then revisited four years later, where the scope for the theory of *bonding* is radically expanded:

> What we are now contemplating, [...], is the possibility of finding bonding across texts written between three and fourteen years apart, solely because of the mental concordances of the authors' retained records of the texts they had read, which in turn were written in the light of *their* author's mental concordances, which (perhaps) included sentences drawn from a common primary source. (Hoey 1995: 90, author's highlights)

While this very clearly links-in with the work done by Quillian during the 1960s, Hoey here merely describes what has been observed. It is very much like the input material presented to the TLC. Yet the basis is laid for the radical step which moves away from the observed bonding both intra- and intertextual to an explanation of how the writers' *mental concordances* come into being. This development happened in the following decade, to culminate in 2005.[2]

In his book *Lexical Priming*, Hoey sets out to explain the particular types of patterns described by corpus linguists: *collocation, colligation* and *semantic preference*. Right at the start, Hoey (2005: 7) says that "collocation is pervasive" and that "any explanation for the pervasiveness of collocation has to be psychological, as ... [it is] a psychological concept". Hoey therefore elects *priming* as the most appropriate concept and it is here where one finds the only brief reference to Neely. Pace-Sigge (2013) then described in detail why the concept of priming is evidentially the most suitable route to explain these phenomena. The core idea of lexical priming is described as follows:

> Every time we use a word, and every time we encounter it anew, the experience either reinforces the *priming* by confirming an existing association between the word and its co-texts and contexts, or it weakens the priming, if the encounter introduces the word in an unfamiliar context or co-text. (Hoey 2005: 9, author's highlights)

It must be added Hoey refers to not just of words but "words or sets of words" or "word sequences"—thus making a link to what Sinclair (1991) defines as *lexical item*. Crucially, all primings are both domain specific and genre specific.[3] The full list of ten "priming hypotheses" can be found in Hoey (2005: 13). Here, however, the focus will be on three patterns mentioned above, as they seem to be the most relevant in the context of both Quillian's past work and current AI developments.

Figure 3.2 gives a highly simplified example of how collocations work: one would, of course, have to look at ever-larger deposits of word usage[4] in different situations to get the best possible overview of the existing collocates and how strong the actual lines of activation would be. It does demonstrate, however, how reinforcement learning is supposed to work. The more often a system sees WORD in the neighbourhood of semantic-field items like *mouth, tongue* or *write*; the more often it is preceded by the articles *a* or *the*, the stronger the reinforcement. Also, through

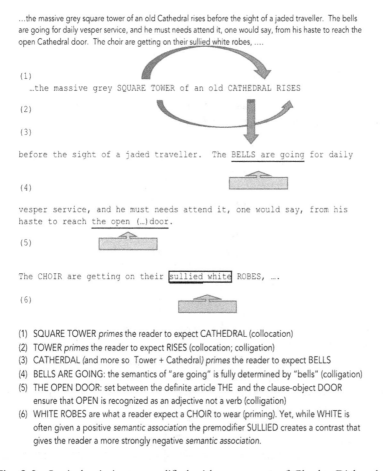

...the massive grey square tower of an old Cathedral rises before the sight of a jaded traveller. The bells are going for daily vesper service, and he must needs attend it, one would say, from his haste to reach the open Cathedral door. The choir are getting on their sullied white robes, ...

(1)
    ...the massive grey SQUARE TOWER of an old CATHEDRAL RISES

(2)

(3)

before the sight of a jaded traveller. The BELLS are going for daily

(4)

vesper service, and he must needs attend it, one would say, from his haste to reach the open (...)door.

(5)

The CHOIR are getting on their sullied white ROBES, ...

(6)

(1) SQUARE TOWER *primes* the reader to expect CATHEDRAL (collocation)
(2) TOWER *primes* the reader to expect RISES (collocation; colligation)
(3) CATHERDAL (and more so Tower + Cathedral) *primes* the reader to expect BELLS
(4) BELLS ARE GOING: the semantics of "are going" is fully determined by "bells" (colligation)
(5) THE OPEN DOOR: set between the definite article THE and the clause-object DOOR ensure that OPEN is recognized as an adjective not a verb (colligation)
(6) WHITE ROBES are what a reader expect a CHOIR to wear (priming). Yet, while WHITE is often given a positive *semantic association* the premodifier SULLIED creates a contrast that gives the reader a more strongly negative *semantic association*.

Fig. 3.2 Lexical priming exemplified with an excerpt of Charles Dickens' *The Mystery of Edwin Drood*

such reinforcement, there will be a stronger expectation that WORD will appear with such items. Yet the point is that machines are neither sentient and nor have they got expectations. This is where statistical probabilities (a *Mutual Information* score is just one of many possible options) come in: a machine can give predictions as to the degree of likelihood that *WORD* appears with any other word. To put it in another way—it describes how strongly WORD prefers the company of that other word and how strongly it disprefers ("shuns" in the terminology of Xiao) such company. We can therefore observe strong relations with WORD and *spoken* or *written* yet WORD and *steel* or *bell* are rather dispreferred. This does not, however, mean that these never co-occur—there are sentences like this: "List of words formed using letters of the Word 'steel'" from a website which gives advice to Scrabble players. Or this: "Bell. Word forms: plural **bells**" which has been taken from the Collins Dictionary. However, statistically these co-occurrences are far less likely than WORD with *said*. A further factor has to be taken into account: WORD is highly frequent, as is *written*—whereas *bell* is not.

Pace-Sigge (cf. 2013: 15) demonstrates that the act *of* colligation itself refers to a psychological process described, in rather general terms, by the German philosopher Wundt as such: "Since A has, a thousand times over, been followed immediately by a, and B by b, the mind argues that A will in future always be attended by a and B by b …" (Wundt 1862, quoted in Titchener 1922: 351). Priming and *colligation* are actually something we have demonstrated earlier (see Fig. 2.1)—though it was not at that stage explained. Hoey orients his definition of colligation towards Halliday's use—i.e. "the relation [held] between a word and a grammatical pattern" (2005: 43). Based on this, colligation is defined by him as follows:

1. the grammatical company a word or word sequence keeps (or avoids keeping) either within its own group or at a higher rank;
2. the grammatical functions preferred or avoided by the group in which the word or word sequence participates; and
3. the place in a sequence that a word or word sequence prefers (or avoids) (Hoey 2005: 43).

Hoey had earlier said that "every word is primed to occur in (or avoid) certain grammatical positions and … functions; these are its colligations" (2005: 13); looking back at the example shown in Fig. 2.1, we can see how the uses of words like *of*, *so* or *to* appear to follow a pattern of occurrence, position and function that can be described as their *colligation pattern*. Such a pattern is explained by priming—the trigger words in the context and co-text. Thus, we can determine that one particular usage structure of *to* is as a *preposition* while another is as the *to-Infinitive*. Going beyond the early idea of bonding, Michael Hoey indicates a primacy of the *lexis* in language, going as far as saying that there is no such thing as "one grammar"—only an accumulation of usage patterns:

> What we count as grammar is the accumulation and interweaving of primings of the most common sounds, syllables and words of the language. So grammar is, in such terms, the sum of the collocates, colligations and semantic associations of words like *is*, *was*, *the*, *a* and *of*, syllables like *ing*, *er* and *ly* and sounds like [t] (at the end of syllables) and [s] and [z] (likewise at the end of syllables). (Hoey 2005: 159)

Grammar, thus, would be based on what is found to be the "usual" or "normal" form encountered. This definition does not explain where it comes from; however, it is a lot closer to the probabilistic model (see Sect. 3.5).

A third key notion of the theory of *lexical priming* is that of *semantic association*. This is a further development of the notion of *semantic preference* and *semantic prosody*,[5] a concept first described by John Sinclair (1987) and Bill Louw (1993), and further developed by Michael Stubbs (1995). According to Louw, certain features of a word are fixed through the environment in which they occur. Thus, as Stubbs demonstrates, the word *cause* is found in over 90% of its uses referring to something unpleasant. While the idea of *connotation* seems to cover something similar (things have a "positive" or a "negative" connotation), *semantic prosody* goes further as it highlights that a large number of words in use have an underlying, subconscious prosody that, according to Louw, only became visible once computers made large-scale concordancing possible.

There has been, indeed, some criticism of the concept, namely by Whitsitt (2005) who highlighted that semantic prosody appears to ignore the minority of cases where its prosodic nature is neutral or in opposition to the prosody claimed for it. Hoey says that, in order to accommodate this criticism and go beyond a sheer positive–negative dichotomy as well as for reasons of clarity, he has settled on the term "semantic association". Furthermore, as *lexical priming* focusses on the psychological element of word choice, it is deemed suitable to name a phenomenon that cannot simply be explained through collocation alone. Hoey therefore defines *semantic association* thus:

> [semantic association] exists when a word or word sequence is associated in the mind of a language user with a semantic set or class, some members of which are also collocates for that user. (2005: 24)

This allows Hoey to link semantic association to negative prosody ("budge"), positive prosody ("young"), neutral associations (number) and exceptions that come from creative language use ("blinding sun"). Furthermore, he describes that *semantic association* can be particularly affected by local collocations that might not appear in an average corpus or act as a complimentary (or, conversely, discourteous) complements to words or word sequences—"bright young men and women" is the example given. It has been found that the sequence "young men and women" is always preceded by a form of compliment in US defence speeches—cf. Hoey (2005: 19).

Figures 3.3 and 3.4 give a schematic demonstration of how priming can be detected in a randomly chosen text. Some of the claims made in Sect. 3.2 are then checked against the evidence. The perfect set-up would be to check Dickens' story against material from other nineteenth-century writers. However, present-day readers may have different primings and therefore, the BNC-F (British fiction of the twentieth century) was chosen to check the concordances for evidence of *collocation, colligation* and *semantic association.*

It is important to highlight that Michael Hoey insisted that lexical primings cannot ever be seen as a fixed, inflexible system. There can be *cracks in primings*—where a prime is no longer matched by the expected target word, or where learners are primed by their L1 and then encounter a different meaning for the same or similar item in the L2 they hope to acquire. Such cracks can eventually lead to complete shifts in primings—as we have demonstrated above with the example of "mistress". "Wireless" (then: radio, now: the wire-free links between computing devices and their accessories) or "gay" (then: carefree, lively, now: almost exclusively taking the US slang use of homosexual) are further examples. Moreover, priming also accounts for creativity or imaginative writing, as users can deliberately break primings, with the effect being humour, ambiguity or a new meaning. Any single public event, advertising campaign or successful creative output might be instrumental to bring this about.[7] Significantly, a direct connection between Quillian's concept for

(1) Looking at near-collocates, there are no cathedrals linked to TOWER – there is, however, CHURCH (note, also, the connection of BELL and TOWER):

L1	Centre	R1	R2	R3
THE	TOWER	OF	THE	THE
WHITE	TO 'S	AND	BQUO	AND
BELL		EQUO	LONDON	EQUO
IVORY		WAS	HE	TO
CHURCH		THE	WAS	HE
GARDEN		TO	IT	IN
CO OL		BLOCK	HOETH	AS
GREAT		SHE	AND	WAS
CLOCK		HE	IN	CHURCH

(2) TOWER is clearly linked to be followed by a lemma of RISE:

m the coast you could see the dock tower, tall and elegant, rising out of the
een high fields, and saw the church tower rising among leafless trees and t
straight up into the air and the dark tower of the church rising above a clust
ly sign of human habitation was the tower of St Hilary church rising out of th
his temple is to be found on a great tower of black adamant rising out of the
hen it can't be explained. Check the tower yourself, Sir Robert, you know it

(4) "Bells are going" is still an idiomatic phrase, though a lot less frequent as "bells are ringing" or "bells are tolling". Both, however, are bound by the –ing form (stationary bells are not typically occurring):

tly upon the town then, and the bells were going for the morning work.
towards St. Mary's. "Why, the bells are going for service; there must be

(6) WHITE is typically preceded by positive words like *snow, pure, great, clean*. There is no occurrence of "sullied white".
SULLIED, by contrast, is extremely rare. While it carries a strong *negative semantic association* demonstrated by the negative words to the left and right to it, it is never employed as an adjective. This points to Dickens' usage being a creative breaking of the core primings in order to direct the reader's attention.

this; I rely on you to see that my name is not sullied by reason of this hare-brained scheme.
gloriously for king and country — was sullied by the fact that my brother had perished
sparkling fresh water and grassy banks being sullied twice daily by the flotsam and jetsam of
me, but he, I fear, will be cut off from himself, sullied, put down completely by all the conflict
marked the end of her parents' lives, sad and sullied by the separations she had lived
nomads. Naturally, d'Arquebus Senior never sullied his own hands — or his eyes
accuracy. Not because the Harlequin man had sullied Meh'Lindi in Jaq's eyes, oh no, no
&bquo;You were right, Pao-yu. All streams are sullied. Nothing is ch'ing… nothing pure.
. &bquo;And that line must never be defiled or sullied.&equo; &bquo;Yes,&equo; said
which never has to be written, which is never sullied with a definite shape, which never
air, but it didn't cleanse him inside. He still felt sullied by what he'd had to do — to
were in the house. So far, Lucien had not sullied his art by performing to music, but he
the kind of victim? This girl was poor and sullied.&equo; &bquo;Do you look for reason

Fig. 3.3 Lexical priming claims in Fig. 3.1 checked against occurrence patterns in the BNC Fiction

a *TLC* and Hoey's ***lexical priming*** can be made when it comes to the disambiguation of polysemous items. Hoey describes how his so-called drinking hypothesis achieves this. One must imagine the cramped cockpit of a plane flying through turbulence. The pilot wants to have a sip

Imagine a machine has to learn how strong the links between words are by focusing on each node and considering each single word four or five words to both the left and the right of this node. These would be the *collocates*, the habitual or characteristic co-occurrence patterns of words.

L5	L4	L3	L2	L1	*node*	R1	R2	R3	R4	R5
TONGUE	WOULDN'T	GET	ROUND	THE	WORD	OR	MY	MOUTH	WOULDN'T	OPEN
AND	CAN	WRITE	DOWN	A	WORD	OR	TWO	FEW	WILL	TURN
LEFT	AND	STILL	NOT	A	WORD	OUT	OF	MR. P	MISS G.	WAS
SO	SAID	POIROT	THE	FRENCH	WORD	CLOSEST	IN	SOUND	TO	THE
IT	THERE	IS	NO	LAST	WORD	HE	WROTE	AND	MISS G.	SEIZING

This seems to indicate that the node WORD has a preference for ARTICLE (A / THE) directly before it; the conjunction OR directly after it. We can also find, nearby, words that fit into the semantic field —TONGUE, SOUND, MOUTH or WRITE / WROTE.

Were we to upscale this and look at all the words in a novel (say: 100,000) or a library or a collection on the internet (millions, billions or trillions of words) this can no longer be done by hand, but has to be resolved statistically. One such method is to test for *Mutual Information or MI*. The following is taken from Richard Xiao's (nd) slides: **MI** is -

- A measure of collocational strength
- The higher the MI score, the stronger the link between two items
- MI score of 3.0 or higher to be taken as evidence that two items are collocates
- The closer to 0 the MI score gets, the more likely it is that the two items co-occur by chance
- A negative MI score indicates that the two items tend to shun each other
- There are variations how the MI is being calculated. See the footnote below for the formula most statistical software tools use.

Fig. 3.4 Collocational statistics and "strong links" for WORD in a random sample of the BNC Fiction sub-corpus[6]

of water from his plastic glass but has **a problem drinking**. In the film *Airplane*, this is turned into a panic-inducing joke by the mere change of word order (=a change of word classes), as the stewardess tells a concerned passenger that the pilot has **"a drinking problem"**. With reference to this example, Hoey explains that, where a word is polysemous, each of their particular word senses must necessarily prefer its own set of collocations, semantic associations and/or colligations. The other sense will tend to avoid these. Furthermore, there is a preference pattern, so that one word-sense is more dominant than the other, rarer word-sense (cf. Hoey 2005: 82). Where such preferences do not occur, a temporary break in primings will be the result which can be deliberate.

Since the publication of his book, the theory has been applied in a number of different ways. Hoey himself looked at the issue of lexical priming and creativity (e.g. Hoey 2008) and, in various talks and papers, at lexical priming and second-language learning, or lexical priming in languages other than English. Looking at languages other than English has also been the focus of Jantunen and Brunni (2013) and Jantunen (2017), who extended the lexical priming hypotheses to include morphology. Pace-Sigge (2013, 2017) has looked at evidence of lexical priming in spoken English; Patterson (2016, 2018) at metaphor use in connection with lexical priming. Details can be found by consulting Pace-Sigge and Patterson (2017): this volume looks at applications and latter advances of the lexical priming theory that covers a large and diverse set of topics.

3.3   SPREADING ACTIVATION, INFERENCE AND FRAME FINDING

3.3.1   Introduction

As we have seen in Chapter 2, *spreading activation* is a way to describe how items can be retrieved from a memory. Consequently, where the activation links are stronger, retrieval is faster. In order to create stronger links, a fact highlighted by Loftus and Collins, the node and the corresponding section of the network (or other node) must have been reinforced through frequent connection; in Sect. 3.2, it was pointed out that *priming* comes from being repeatedly exposed to the same collocations, colligations, etc. This provides a link to *machine learning* through the concept of *RL* or *Reinforcement Learning*: here, it is machines who firm up activation links through repeat exposure (and links that have not got this kind of exposure are, consequently, weaker).

The iPhone has "only" turned ten years old in 2017, and most people in high-income countries and many people in medium-income countries find themselves in a world of hyper-information—be it what friends are eating or where acquaintances are holidaying, 24-hour news cycles or books of any length. These are available anytime and, thanks to mobile technology, anywhere. Likewise, every owner of a smartphone has become a constant producer of information—whether by simply clicking on a "like" button or commenting on any given event or taking and posting of photographs, videos and audio recordings online. While some are aware that this is only a stage along the way where *big data* plays an ever-more important role in all areas of life, it becomes increasingly difficult to comprehend that all these developments are fairly recent. In fact, simply watching a TV tech programme from as little as four or five years ago presents us with "new tech" and "predictions for future technological advances" which can already seem quite quaint and outdated. With all this in mind, it should be no surprise that a large number of people tend to have a foreshortened idea of history that is very much focussed on the now. This kind of disposition might make people forget that the current technologies we are able to access or which will soon be widely available had quite a long lead-in time to be developed. This time-span appears to be rather long in the framework of ever-increasing computing power; rather long when considering the technological tools and applications available to a large market of consumers in 2018. However, the 1980s and 1990s were the crucial decades in the development of the key technologies discussed in this book.[8]

In the words of Fritz Lehmann, "When the field of *AI* emerged in the 1960's, semantic *networks* quickly became important (based primarily on Quillian's network program for word meanings) and they have been in the mainstream of AI ever since" (Lehmann 1992: 7). We have seen in Chapter 2 that Quillian's work has formed the basis for two particular strands of research—one being psycholinguists, which has now been covered in depth. The other is the field of *artificial intelligence*. In his 1986 PhD thesis, Peter Norvig (who would go on to become Director of Research at Google Inc.) gave the most compelling reason as to why AI researchers should be interested in how the mind works:

> There are a number of reasons why AI researchers should be concerned with results in psychology. From a scientific view, one of the goals of AI is to better understand human cognition. From the engineering point of view, humans are the best, and only, example of working intelligent systems and thus are worth examining. Finally, because language is a means of communicating mental concepts between humans, understanding language requires an understanding of human mental processes. (Norvig 1987: 44f.)

One may find the assertion of "humans are the only intelligent system" debateable now. This does not, however, hinder the assertion that humans are, of all possible intelligent systems, the ones best understood.

3.3.2   *The Lack of* Understanding *in Quillian's* Semantic Network *and* Inference Models *to Overcome This Drawback*

No idea, no theory is ever perfect, nor can it be implemented or applied directly in real life: there will be setbacks, garden paths that lead nowhere; there will be brilliant insights that prove to be plain wrong. In the following, it will be shown how Quillian's ideas were adopted, modified and later improved to such a degree that machines indeed could start to fulfil the tasks Quillian had envisioned for them.

In discussing earlier research in the field of AI, both Wilensky (1983) and Norvig (personal communication) single out Quillian's work which, as Norvig points out, appeared rather primitive by the 1980s but had been state of the art 20 years before. Fritz Lehmann describes it fittingly as follows:

> Quillian considered the full meaning of a word to be the sum total of all the structure built by recursively substituting for each word its definition. In a semantic network, substituting the defining net of a concept for the node representing the concept itself is, in fact, a graph-grammar substitution of a complex graph for a simple one. Such a substitution is an increase in granularity and detail, a semantic 'zooming in'. (Lehmann 1992: 29)

The one major characteristic Quillian's theory demonstratively lacks is *understanding*—there is no clear distinction between words (treated as single nodes) and the concepts (or *units of meaning*) these represent. Yet this "blindness" (a clear drawback) can also be seen as a feature that enhances processing speed. Quillian, like his then-colleague Sheldon Klein, is viewed as the first to develop the idea of the *semantic web*[9] (see, amongst others, Noordman-Vonk 1979; Norvig 1987; Sowa 1987; Hobbs et al. 1988; Shastri 1992; Steyvers and Tenenbaum 2005). As a consequence, rather than processing ever-more complex entities, the system relies on a *memory network* within which related entities can be retrieved. This, as we saw in Chapter 2, facilitates *word-sense disambiguation* but also, according to Norvig (1987), *property composition*. This means that a given node (or word) can have both superordinate and subordinate links, they can be contrasted and prototypical forms or examples can be compared. Furthermore, the TLC model allows for *anaphoric reference resolution*. This means that the system back-references to ideas mentioned earlier in the text. Usually, these are linked through the use of proper names, full definite descriptions and pronouns. Beyond these facilities, it is a highly automated system, where the search procedure itself is fully autonomous. Crucially, "[p]rocessing is based on semantic relationships. Syntax serves a secondary role" (Norvig 1986: 47). Overall, this highlights why this model formed such a resilient basis for developing utterance-comprehending algorithms: the reliance on a memory-only, syntax-blind and autonomously searching-and-retrieving model that is helped in its quest to comprehend language demands by working out anaphoric references offers a relatively fast and stable foundation. For

Norvig though, the model is limited when one tries to upscale it; also, while such a machine can comprehend "lawyer's client" (Quillian's own example), Norvig reckons that the original system would struggle with "the lawyer's new client" the reason being the system's non-dependency on syntactic rules. This does not mean that the system cannot be updated and suitably extended to fulfil the demand to cover a greater range of needs. The concept of spreading activation does, indeed, live on and is constantly developed. The following just give a broad set of examples from this decade—work by people like Brian Harrington, of the Oxford University Computing Lab (2010) focussing on relatedness as demonstrated in semantic networks; Teufl and Kraxberger (2011), who aimed to extract semantic knowledge from Twitter; Ronan Mac an tSaoir, a researcher of IBM's *Watson Group*, used spreading activation in 2014 to evaluate and improve ontologies; or Ercan Canhasi's *GSolver* which, in 2016, looked to solve word-association puzzles in the Albanian language. Still, in each of these cases, a move away from the original work is necessitated. Quillian's model allows for forward- and back-referencing; recognising coherence markers in the process and therefore identifying that "he" is mentioned in reference to "John" and not in reference to "Jane".

According to Yu and Simmons (1988), the idea of *marker passing* was introduced by Ross Quillian [1966] (1968), though not much attention was paid to this concept until the 1980s. Carroll and Charniak (1991: 69) provide the following definition: "Marker-passing uses a breadth-first search to find paths between concepts in an associative network made up of concepts and their part-subpart relations". Yu and Simmons point out that the renewed focus on Quillian's work was due to developments in hardware architectures, which actually facilitate a genuine form of parallelism which allows the addition of new pieces of knowledge without degrading (slowing) the performance of the whole system. The difficulty that is presented, in particular by the use of more complex sentence structures, is how to link items in a text that appear to have no obvious semantic links. This is the concrete issue of *inference*—how B can be inferred from A. Yet, in order to *infer* anything, a system, whether human or digital, has to have a minimum level of information. The less direct the link between A and B, the greater the need for further information. It appears obvious that this presents an obvious hurdle for Quillian's original approach, as the focus is of text-inherent information. Cohesive elements are, therefore, easily integrated. What about this example however?

> *John* walked into the **shop**.
> Returning <u>home</u>, his partner chided *him* for forgetting **bread**.

When focussing solely on text data, it is clear that *him* refers to *John*. Yet, how does one make a connection between **shop** and **bread**? This seems to be very simple for a human listener, who uses daily experience to understand that people go into shops in order to buy stuff and this includes food like bread. Thus, information not stated in the actual text can be *inferred* because it is implied: the listener clearly makes use of a parallel system that provides this knowledge without recourse to text semantics. A machine, however, would have to have such knowledge in order to make the correct inference. In larger texts, inference might be assisted by the fact that **bread** and **shop** are collocates. Yet, **bread** is consumed at **home**. In fact, that collocational link might even be stronger.[10] It is at this point that Peter Norvig directly compares Quillian's TLC with his own "teachable language understander"—FAUSTUS. The difference is described thus:

> FAUSTUS has a better way of combining informatics from syntax and semantics. Both TLC and FAUSTUS suggested inference by spreading markers from all components of the input, and looking for collisions. The difference is that the TLC used syntactic relations only as a filter to eliminate certain suggestions while Faustus incorporates the meaning of these relations into the representation before spreading markers. (Norvig 1987: 125)

Apparently, source-based inference by itself is possible yet might not be sufficient. Therefore, unlike the unconstrained approach used by Quillian, there is a need to use certain constraints. One solution, already suggested by Marvin Minski, is that of a *frame* (also referred to as *script* or *scheme*). Robert Wilensky describes an earlier version of FAUSTUS:

> When FAUSTUS has an input, it first looks at instantiated frames to see if the input elaborates one of them, and then looks for frames that are indexed under the input. For example, frames suggesting the cause of an event are likely to be invoked by this process. FAUSTUS's determination process then looks for verification of these frames. Supporting evidence includes the previous mention of one of these frames or of their constituents. Thus FAUSTUS checks the story representation and other invoked frames for corroborating items. (Wilensky 1983: 403)

This would mean that a system has access to sources beyond the text and can instrumentalise those to have a more precise understanding. In other words, can infer from those two sentences above that John entered the shop with the plan to buy things (shop -> buy things) and that his partner had expected that one of these things was bread (expectation broken -> forgetting; response: chiding). One might also add the frame that food is needed by humans and therefore they have it in their home. A possible solution is of course to present the system with each possible frame and therefore any kind of discourse can be understood and processed. This is the kind of approach developed by Wilensky (1982), Norvig (1983), Charniak (1986) as well as Charniak and Goldman (1988). Here, the authors defined *frame* as such: "Let us assume that all words in English have one or more word senses as their meaning, that these word senses correspond to frames and that any particular word instance has as its meaning exactly one of these senses" (Charniak and Goldman 1988: 89).

This, for obvious reasons, hits the harsh wall of reality that there are possibly an infinite number of frames. As a result, a number of proto-typical frames would have to be constructed and an understander would then have to draw inferences depending on the statistical likelihood that a discourse is more fitting for one frame than for another.[11]

Norvig (1987) describes the key approaches to resolve this issue in the 1980s. He makes the caveat, however, that in the attempt to create *story understanding* machines, the focus has been very much on the under-standing, while the key must be the domain—a story that a reader reads is very different from news that an audience watches on TV. Norvig therefore points to the importance of *story grammar*. "Story Analysis programs are interesting because they can provide insight into the structure of stories, the notion of coherence, and the interaction between events, goals, and plans" (Norvig 1992: 1). Thus "understanding" of such texts should help to retrieve useful information and improve key-wording techniques—something Norvig (1989b) pointed towards when describing how to build "a large lexicon with Lexical Network Theory".

The idea to investigate how stories work in order to create digital understanding machines has a long pedigree which clearly influenced Norvig (see, e.g., Charniak 1972 or Wilensky 1978, 1982). Expanding on this concept, he proposes that a set of constraints is to be imposed so that inference can be aided:

[N]atural language texts are almost always ambiguous to some extent, so a unique solution to the constraint problem cannot be achieved. Instead, a least cost or most likely interpretation must somehow be computed, using heuristics that combine evidence from various sources while limiting the number of choices considered. (Norvig 1989a: 571)

In order to have such constraints, a relevant knowledge base is set up alongside the purely text-based sources used. This base should carry a set of annotation rules as described:

1. define terms and describe the domain
2. represent meanings in the text and indicate ambiguities
3. represent meanings as derived from the text (Norvig 1987: 53).

As becomes clear, this goes beyond the mere rows and rows of text input. Instead, we have a system that integrates part of the indexing cat-alogue (found traditionally in libraries) and a part-of-speech (POS) tag-ger that is both reliant on an external dictionary (2) and cross-references with how words are employed in the actual text (3). The relevance of this is quite apparent: any system that has this additional information will be aware if the text at hand was written in 2017 rather than in 1717 and that the genre is "transcription of a physics lecture" rather than a "satirical poem" with words like "unity" having different meaning values in either. In other words, a more rounded semantic annotation system is brought into being. Crucially, Norvig set out to create a basic plat-form in the FAUSTUS system that was stable to the point that no ad hoc further rules or changes to rules could be implemented (these would simply have satisfied the demands of one particular example fed into the machine). This means that the machine can inference without top-down control. Yet even then there are drawbacks, some similar to the TLC. For FAUSTUS, all chains are of equal value; it cannot distinguish: everything has equal relevance. Therefore, the machine would not be able to decide which piece is more interesting or more usual; it would also not know if one or more of its own rules are in conflict with another. Still, Charniak (1986) and Norvig (1987) found that "most marker-passer systems have found many more bad paths, suggesting incorrect schemas, than good ones. [A possible solution to raise] the good/bad path ratio can [is] by exploiting probability information" (Carroll and Charniak 1991: 69).

Hobbs and colleagues (1988) claim that their own system, TACITUS is close to FAUSTUS, yet more efficient. They speak of *"abduction* to be *inference* to the best explanation" (Hobbs et al. 1988: 1). TACITUS stands for *The Abductive Commonsense Inference Text Understanding System,* and "common sense" in "understanding" was a main concern Norvig had hoped to address, too. Both systems are constraint-based, and TACITUS aims to be a pragmatic *understander:* abduction being a principle of logic, where "the major premise is certain and the minor only probable, so that the conclusion has only the probability of the minor" (OED). Consequently, it is directed to give the most plausible explanation, even if a final proof cannot be supplied. In the author's own words:

> Interpretation in general may be viewed as abduction. When we look out the window and see a tree waving back and forth, we normally assume the wind is blowing. There may be other reasons for the tree's motion; for example, someone below window level might be shaking it. But most of the time the most economical explanation coherent with the rest of what we know will be that the wind is blowing. This is an abductive explanation. (Hobbs et al. 1988: 60)

The authors made clear that the concept of *redundancy* had been well described by linguists before they integrated it into their processes, and given that the declared aim is to create an efficient constraint on the possible options what can be inferred, this appears to be a sensible route to take. Hobbs et al. (c. 1988: 13f.) describe that their system has a scheme of abductive inference with four features:

1. It should be possible for goal expressions to be assumable, at varying costs.[12]
2. There should be the possibility of making assumptions at various levels of specificity.
3. There should be a way of exploiting the natural redundancy of texts to yield more economic proofs.
4. Whenever an assumption is made, it should first be checked for consistency.

This then provides a logic-based constraint system that is meant to answer the issue of text-pragmatics. While Quillian's model was text-based, looking at inference clues both intratextual and intertextual with very limited options to take recourse to the "knowledge base" (the dictionary definitions), the hardware developments achieved in the 1980s meant that parallel computing was no longer a desirable concept but a viable option.

3.3.3   *More Recent* Inference Models *Using* Frame Semantics

Move forward ten years, the processing model presented by Harabagiu and Moldovan (1997) refines the degree of inference yet more through a marker passing system referred to as *marker propagation*. This process is described in detail by Dekai Wu (1989): "the [potential] advantages of marker-passing over local connectionist techniques for associative inference are (1) the ability to differentiate variable bindings, and (2) reduction in the search space and/or number of processing elements" (Wu 1989: 574). This is a constraint system atop the spread activation first proposed by Quillian which is based upon a probabilistic analysis. Harabagiu and Moldovan managed to make use of the much better computing powers available since the late 1980s. They used WordNet 1.5—which, in 1997, had 168,217 words organised in 91,591 concepts. This creates a total of 259,812 nodes that can be activated. They claim that this covers the "large majority of English words. [And] believe that a methodology like the one presented here for text inference can improve not only word-sense disambiguation, discourse analysis and other critical natural language tasks" (Harabagiu and Moldovan 1997: 208).

Moving on by another 15 years, it might be useful to look at some work undertaken by computational linguists, namely Dipanjan Das and colleagues. Originating with the work of Charles Fillmore in the early 1980s, the concept of *frame semantics* was adopted for *FrameNet* in 2003:

> a linguistic resource storing considerable information about lexical and predicate-argument semantics in English. (…) it suggests—but does not formally define—a semantic representation that blends representations familiar from word-sense disambiguation and semantic role labelling. (Das et al. 2014: 10).

Norvig (1983 amongst others) had highlighted that, in order to understand a story, the understander needs to have domain awareness; in other words, needs to have knowledge of the goal of the text received. Das et al. build on that, providing "targets" so that the parser can identify their frames, which is done through statistical modelling. Thus, the level of constraint rests with the parser. The developers say that for "frame identification we make use of frame-evoking lexical units" (2014: 22). Such *lexical units* can easily number a dozen words per node; also, in order to cope with polysemy and homonymy, each lexical unit can be linked to a number of frames. As we have shown above, inference model understanders have struggled with issues like mapping overlap or contradictory results where details of different frames send the system, quite literally, up a garden path. A stronger, more robust system of probabilistic checks had been mooted and this system has been further developed here, where several probabilistic models have been trained on the basis of the full annotated version of the FrameNet lexicon, using a semantic parsing network that makes abductions that cover the not given pieces of information so as to predict the most likely *frame*. In their presentation, Das et al. show that their original model could even be improved by being semi-supervised (therefore no longer fully automated)—yet their model still managed to be more accurate than the benchmark (from 2007) fully supervised model. Additionally, Das et al. have created an "argument identification model, trained using maximum conditional log-likelihood, [that] unifies the traditionally separate steps of detecting and labelling arguments" (2014: 49). It can be seen that this provides a highly evolved platform for text understanding. The area most prominently described by Norvig as undeveloped by Quillian's model is being addressed here, and the key lies in advanced statistical models that are applied here. Yet, despite being quite successful—the frame prediction lies between 85 and 91%— this is far from perfect, certainly when measured against the total number that can be expected to appear in a typical text. It also still requires a level of supervision. The most obvious drawback lies, however, in its reliance on FrameNet—something implied by the authors, who originally undertook tests with FrameNet 1.3 and then published their results on the basis of the larger FrameNet 1.5. This means that, where FrameNet is blind to certain words and concepts, it cannot provide reliable information to build frames; it also means that issues like language-change and variation (based on domain, genre, speech community) create a natural hindrance for this system of frame-semantic parsing to be universally employed.

As will be shown in Sect. 3.4, the models developed by Harabagiu and Moldovan or Das et al. continue to be questioned, revised and developed further in order to reach ever-higher levels of reliability.

As can be seen, the original concept of *spreading activation* within a *semantic web* had become a suitable basis for further developments; however, it proved insufficient to deal with more complex sentences, nor could the issue of semantic meaning be addressed in a satisfactory way. While Quillian had implemented a simple way to integrate *Inference*, this mainly consisted of linking one word (*node*) to another *node* that appears either before or after it. This in itself had been advantageous: the spreading is not linear but allows for expanding circles of linkable nodes. While helpful for processing speed and capacity, it brought with it the necessitated restriction that all "knowledge" available to the digital comprehension set-up was limited to the material input. The one knowledge base that Quillian had made provision for was the reference source—a single dictionary in his case—yet the technology of the 1960s and early 1970s simply did not allow for fast enough parallel processing to go much beyond the source-based activation model. The early 1980s finally saw the provision of the necessary hardware to run data processing at the required speed and in parallel, which opened the route to make use of far more complex and greatly expanded knowledge bases which provided for inferencing in a much more targeted way. Thus, whole schedules and concepts could be linked to each single node—which resulted in a machine that used *spreading activation* to provide statistically robust tools to enable *frame finding*: the process of linking the occurrence frequency and pattern of nodes within their web of more or less strongly activated co-nodes to a particular semantic frame.

3.4 FROM QUILLIAN'S *SPREADING ACTIVATION* TO *EDGE PRUNING*

3.4.1 Introduction

As pointed out in Sect. 3.3, direct reference to Quillian's work can be seen to recede as newer, more advanced approaches are available; yet amid most of the research undertaken globally, implicit and explicit echoes of Quillian's work remain poignant.[13] Yet, why the language might have changed, the projects described in this section all explicitly reference back to Quillian's, Collins' and Loftus' work on *spreading activation*.

3.4.2 Spreading Activation *Algorithms in the Twenty First Century*

This section covers all the most recent uses of *spreading activation* which make direct reference to Quillian's work.

Currently, the issue of *word-sense disambiguation* (WSD) continues to be seen as one of the most critical and difficult to solve technical problems, a so-called *AI complete*. While semi-supervised and fully supervised systems can produce excellent results (and set a bench mark), the aim is to have a system in place that can resolve ambiguities without manual intervention.

Harrington (2010) pointed out that WordNet, a key tool in determining *semantic relatedness,* has a specific drawback: it measures relatedness by the distance between terms, yet, as he says, its hierarchical taxonomic structure can lead to inefficiencies. It can, for example, result in "… terms such as car and bicycle being close in the network, but terms such as car and gasoline being far apart" (Harrington 2010: 357).[14] This system clearly does not mirror how such terms are connected to the human mind and become problematic as it both slow down the recognition and disambiguation process and also prevent reasonable scalability outside the sets of words found in WordNet.

Harrington's aim is to fill the crucial gap he sees between "human intuition" and data harvested from even large corpora. He points out that statistical methods highlight links between words, using vector space or *PageRank* algorithms are very successful—yet they require vast corpora (he cites a research paper that makes use of 1.6 terawords) and offer diminishing returns regardless of how much the corpus size is increased. As a result, Harrington proposes his approach which does not rely on throwing ever-larger data sets at a problem. Instead, he returns to the basic tenets in order to make smarter use of even small data sets (corpora):

> Distinct occurrences of terms and entities are combined into a single node using a novel form of spreading activation (Collins and Loftus, 1975). This combining of distinct mentions produces a cohesive connected network, allowing terms and entities to be related across sentences and even larger units such as documents. Once the network is built, spreading activation is used to determine semantic relatedness between terms. For example, to determine how related *car* and *gasoline* are, activation is given to one of the nodes, say *car*, and the network is "fired" to allow the activation to spread to the rest of the network. The amount of activation received by *gasoline* is then a measure of the strength of the semantic relation between the two terms. (Harrington 2010: 357f.)

If this sounds familiar, it should—this concept has been described in detail above (see, amongst others, Fig. 2.3). Harrington used his system on a single news-story and then asked human evaluators to judge its accuracy: while the result was very respectable, a success rate of 80% accuracy left a sizeable fifth of the text as poorly represented. Still, given that the concept is fully automatic without any manual interference, the issue of scalability certainly is addressed: a machine will be able to produce a larger amount of core semantic networks at a faster speed than any group of humans. Furthermore, the design allows for actualising the existing network—there is an update algorithm that takes into account the relatedness of newly added information and integrates these with the appropriate mappings in the existing framework. This appears to link new nodes in the semantic framework, and Harrington gives the example of *Crosby—Vancouver—Canada*. The links to *Vancouver* and *Canada* should therefore create a stronger link (in his words: "increase the mapping score") to *Sidney Crosby*, an ice hockey player, while decreasing the score to *Bing Crosby*, the singer. Crucially, Harrington demonstrates the relevance of the system even within the framework of present-day data deposits and computation facilities.

Both Szymanski and Duch (2012) and Mac an tSaoir (who is part of IBM's *Watson* group), in 2014, look at statistical analysis of a graph representing interconcept relationships. It appears as if these present the latest successful direct applications of *spreading activation* that can be traced. Both investigations make use of biomedical semantic networks—for obvious reasons as they have been designed to give health researchers maximum access to research data with a minimum of effort. Thus, both make use of the '"Unified Medical Language System" (UMLS)—this is a set of tools, websites and databases created and maintained by the National Library of Medicine, a division of US National Institutes of Health' as Szymanski and Duch describe it. The authors of both research articles point out that, were all concepts and relations combined, an unworkably high total number of relations would be encountered. The UMLS metadata corpus that both employ has the advantage of being tagged, so that the single words or "surface forms" are combined so that they can be found under specific headings, the so-called individual concept IDs (Concept Unique Identifiers, CUIs). What these entail is shown in Table 3.1.

In this way, the *semantic type* acts like a frame, the nodes being all part of a larger concept. The concept thus developed is even more successful than Harrington's: his method enables him to assign a single word-sense for every ambiguous word or surface form in between 82 and 89 out of a 100 cases. Semi-supervised (using just one-fifth of the available data) this rises to 92—which is very close to the fully supervised (and also to the fully human) gold standard.

There are two key areas, however, where this approach meets insurmountable difficulties. The first is the case of *overstimulated nodes*, where a single item can link to too many other nodes. Mac an tSaoir gives the word "retina" as an example in his medical lexicon data—he refers to them as "black hole nodes": these seem to be of no obvious relevance to the document in question, yet they can skewer any results. The second area that is problematic is imbalances or biases:

> (…) for example where a node is unreachable (isolated in the graph), or node degree and node edge-type variation are relatively low, it is less likely that the spreading activation will reflect the meaning of the text. (Mac an tSaoir 2014: 2245)

Readers may remember that the issue of "unreachable nodes" was also highlighted by Harrington who aimed to minimise the impact of such occurrences—still, his experimental machine (2012) had a lower success rate than this one (2014).

3.4.3   *The* Small World Network *as a Modified Spreading Activation System*

In order to achieve the most efficient way to implement a *spreading activation* system is to restrict it. One way—the use of *frames*—has been described. Another technique is restrain, by design, how nodes are

Table 3.1   Surface forms associated with the concept "Heart"[15]

NCI Metathesaurus (Concept Unique Identifier)	UWDA definition	Semantic type	Synonyms Surface form (Text)*
Heart (CUI C0018787)	Organ with cavitated organ parts, which is connected to the systemic and pulmonary arterial and venous trees. Example: there is only one heart	Body part, organ, or organ component	cardiac cardiac structure cor coronary heart hearts heart structure Herz

linked to obtain results more quickly. How this has been approached is described here.

It must be noted that similar concepts have seen a shift in terminology. As mathematical modelling constructions are being taken on to a greater degree, the words activated along the spreading continuum remain to be called *nodes* whereas the links between these nodes are referred to as *edges*. Furthermore, the original model envisaged activation to spread out from a trigger to a set of nodes that are not in a particular (i.e. regular) shape and that does not face any restriction. This is what Steyvers and Tenenbaum (2005) refer to as an "unstructured, arbitrary" form of activation spreading. Factually, this might be a good reflection of the organisation and collection of nodes in a human brain—acquisition and exposure are unplanned, irregular and not aim-oriented. Within a computing system, however, this is not the most efficient way to achieve fast retrieval within the semantic web. One key issue in computing is "cost" it refers to the effort a machine needs to make.[16] Cost is minimised— using less of processing units and memory banks for shorter amounts of time. Even with the enormous advance in processing power, this is relevant—the smaller the cost, the more parallel computations can be carried out, the better the result within a window of time. This is related to what Touretzky (1986) calls the *inheritance system* "a representation system founded on the hierarchical structuring of knowledge". Essentially, the original Quillian concept is an inheritance system. Touretzky (ibid.) describes two problems these systems cannot handle: "reasoning in the presence of true but redundant assertions" and "coping with ambiguity". Above, we have seen how the latter issue had been addressed. The first point, though, is extremely relevant where computing costs (read: obstacles to maximum efficiency) are concerned. If an assertion is true, it will be considered as relevant within a knowledge system. Szymanski and Duch (2012: 183) modify this: "Inheritance along all edges cannot be allowed because not every fact about the world is true or relevant in a given context". This, indeed, is a marked feature in natural language use, where one word or phrase can carry a number of different meanings depending on the context and co-text the word/set of words is found in. The task of a highly proficient system is to be not side-tracked by every logically (true) assertion. As a result, the system does not take into account every available path; instead, only a *small world network model* (cf. Steyvers and Tenenbaum) will be considered. In an unstructured and arbitrary network, nodes could be found spread far apart or equidistant;

in a *small world network*, however, relevant nodes are not necessarily neighbours, yet each node is a neighbour to another node that links (in short steps) to another node in order to reach the node relevant to the initiator. In other words, *activation spreading* does not fire in all directions and with diminishing rates of return, it fires along short stretches. The *small world network model* is probably best described by the concept of "six degrees of separation" where each person can be linked to a random stranger, through links with friends and friends of friends.

Figure 3.5 shows the difference: where the activation spreading between nodes is arbitrary (left), there can be a single (but longer) link, for example 2 to 5. There are short direct links as well, as between 1 and 2, 2 and 3. Alternatively, in the connection 2 to 5 can be via three short steps. However, as every node seems to be linked to a number of nodes enabling various pathways, a lot of noise is created and that can slow down the process. The small world network (right), by contrast, has just two links per node. Thus, the connection from node 1 to node 5 would proceed in small steps via nodes 2, 3 and 4.

A further development was presented by Szymanski and Duch (2012) who propose that the number of nodes will be *pruned*, thus avoiding any *unnecessary inheritance*. They therefore claim that:

> Our algorithm spreads activation from one term to the other, inferring facts not present in the text, but preserving only those facts that improve text classification, avoiding unnecessary inheritance. In this way relevant "pathways of the brain" are discovered. (Szymanski and Duch 2012: 181)

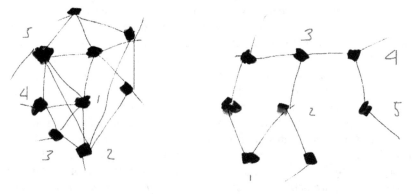

Fig. 3.5 Arbitrary activation spreading (left) versus small world network spreading (right)

They also show that usage of the entire network (the "unpruned" version) does not improve the results they have achieved. The pruning process comes through a set of inhibitions that the algorithm creates. However, it presents a major drawback: while the resulting machine might be efficient, there is little efficiency to get there. The authors describe how there are up to 60 iterations in which the algorithm cuts out the non-relevant pathways. They concede that

> [l]anguage competence at the human level may require detailed neurocognitive models that combine several kinds of memory: recognition, semantic, episodic and short-term working memory, in addition to the iconic spatial and other types of imagery. (Szymanski and Duch 2012: 185)

This, they say, is not practical to recreate. While it can be assumed that competence to use a language results out of a combination of facilities, there is no fully conclusive evidence which tools the human mind employs, whether it involves different types of memory to the same extent, and in how far it requires a certain degree of elasticity. Yet, what cannot fully be recreated in the image of the human mental abilities, digital machines can make up through their advantages in a number of areas where brute computing power can overcome other such shortfalls. For example, more—and more varied—training data, parallel computing and ever-more sophisticated mathematical modelling, in particular, stochastic models. Moreover, while we have seen how ever-more powerful computational tools shrink in size every few years, we may yet have to encounter a massive leap in accuracy of output, to be precise: a quantum leap. The game-changer that a quantum computer might be was something Chris Manning, in his 2017 NLP lectures at Stanford,[17] hinted at.

3.5 SEMANTIC SPACES, LANGUAGE MODELLING AND DEEP NEURAL NETWORKS: TOWARDS UNDERSTANDING ASSISTANTS LIKE GOOGLE GO AND APPLE'S SIRI

3.5.1 Introduction

Over the last dozen years, the model proposed by Quillian continues to be influential as an idea, though its application had to be adopted, as Peter Norvig describes here:

In Quillian's classic TLC, he contrasted two approaches: one is for the programmer to build in knowledge by hand. The second is to augment that knowledge by making assertions, using the language that the system understands. That was state-of-the-art for 1969. In this century, both of those approaches are considered too limited – too hard to scale up to understanding a broad language. Instead, we learn from examples from billions or trillions of published words of text.[18]

However, the practical applications developed rely on mathematical models that are markedly advanced to anything employed by Quillian and his collaborators. Thus, for example, when surveying the developments over the last decade, Collobert and Weston (2008) made no reference to Quillian or his work, yet their proposed training for a *deep neural network* does appear like an updated TLC: instead of a dictionary, the system uses the entirety of *Wikipedia* as its source. Any given input sentence "is processed by several layers of feature extraction. The features in deep layers of the network are automatically trained by backpropagation to be relevant to the task" (Collobert and Weston 2008: 161). There is an element of supervision here (the reference to *backpropagation*). This means that, unlike the use of a single process, the machine goes over the same data several times, with the deeper layers being trained in reference to what earlier extractions have revealed. Within the framework of this book, it is important to note that both the original concept of the 1960s and the contemporary system take into account not only each individual word but they also look at phrases (sequences of words)—both within the text in question and within co-occurrence of any other texts. Therefore, amongst the objectives listed, one finds "named-entity recognition, learning a language model and the task of semantic role-labelling" (ibid.: 160). While the first and the last of these could be construed as by-products of the TLC concept, the notion of "learning a language model" is clearly shared. The *parallel processing* described above is taken one step further, and it has become *multitask learning* where the whole network runs tasks jointly to produce language-processing predictions. The idea of the *semantic net* is also reflected in a particular feature devised by the authors: they use WordNet as one of the knowledge bases to train their system and WordNet provides a 150,000 set of semantic relations (synonyms, homonyms, hypernyms, etc.). Where the input correlates with the database, it is classed as "positive" yet where correlation does not exist, it is "negative"—the latter being a clear drawback that has been addressed since (see below). It also highlights that the authors have tried to devise a system that allows short cuts that are outside the sphere of spreading activation network but can assist it, namely the semantic relations addition.

3.5.2 Statistical Prediction Models

At this point, almost everything deals with *statistical prediction models*.[19] The more likely it is that event B follows event A, and the less likely it is that event C follows event A, the greater the likelihood of A-B: thus, the more accurate the prediction. Some very basic examples are shown in Fig. 3.6.

Clearly, as the capabilities of computing technology expanded, different, more complex and scalable systems have been developed which

Q: "What day is it tomorrow?" A: 100% predictable

Q: "What day is it tomorrow?" A: one-in-seven chance to be correct (14.3%)

Q: "What is tomorrow's date?" A: three-in-four chance to be correct (75.0%). Leap years would have the 29/02.

Fig. 3.6 Predictability examples

would replace earlier, relatively simple prediction systems. The shift can definitely be described as "work smarter, not harder". The original hard-working model was the *Markov Chain Model* (and its adapted off-spring, the *mixed order Markov*). Yet, as Peter Norvig (2011) pointed out, the model is too simplistic and even x amount of runs within a probabilistic Markov chain model cannot reliably predict words in all but the simplest of English sentences. An alternative approach is to feed the machine massive amounts of data—say, 1-billion-word corpora—and then calculate the probability of chunks of words or word clusters (n-grams) occurring. In order to minimise computing time and capacity, one would prefer smaller chunks (bigrams or trigrams) yet, in order to be most useful, N5 grams (a string consisting of five words) are seen as preferable. Still, while being more accurate than Markov chains, this approach would come at the cost of speed and practicability—in particular when ever-larger blocks of words are being calculated. As Mikolov and Zweig (2012) point out: "we have observed that character and sub-word-level language models based on n-gram statistics are very memory inefficient compared to neural networks models". It makes sense, therefore, to employ different approaches. Most crucially, the later models discussed here make use of advanced arithmetic calculations, namely *vector spaces*. The traditional example (see Fig. 3.7) to explain vectors in nature is that of a plane which flies from **A** to **B**, being 1000 km apart (1) with a constant speed of 500 km/h. Thus, a flight time of two hours would be calculated. However, there is headwind (2) which pushes the plane off a straight and direct flight-path. This means there is no direct connection **A** to **B**: **B** can only be reached via **C**, meaning that the resulting total distance is higher than the 1000 given. Thus, instead of (1), the total that needs to be calculated is (2) plus (3).

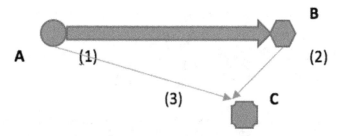

Fig. 3.7 An explanation of vectors

Within language research, Manin and Marcolli say that a Vector Space Model "starts with a large corpus of natural language texts and produces from it a matrix of numbers" (2016: 8). They also highlight that most of the statistical characteristics in such a model do not depend on a particular order (alphabetical, frequency, etc.), but on the relative likelihood in which words can co-occur.

This, indeed, is where the magic of *vector spaces* comes in: items in a language can be assigned a vector representation. Vector representation is the form that enables to create computer programs that do not have to understand any natural language or any nuances: the vector ascribed will indicate whether it is in the neighbourhood to another word; has a preference or dispreference to co-occur with this word; has a relationship to this word, etc. This, to put it another way, is the procedure to allow computer models to mimic the kind of relationships a human language user would draw (in, say, a word-relation task) yet the process is not pre-programmed: the machine will find "natural" relationships. Mikolov et al. (2013) give examples that are either grammatical: syntax (big—bigger; mouse—mice) or general knowledge: semantics (Picasso—painter; Einstein—scientist) or field specific (uranium—plutonium). Therefore, when looking at language, vector arithmetic can be used to calculate each word in relation to another. The direct line A to B would mean that each single word will appear with another single word in 100% of all cases. There are certain words that appear in well over 50 in a 100 cases with another word (I call these *mono-collocates*)—these, however, do not represent a typical relation between words. In a *vector space,* all words in question (a source like "WordNet", etc.) would have to be put in relation to each other: some would indeed have a rather flat link; others, because of their "headwinds", would have a greater magnitude. In other words, a *vector space* is "a group whose elements can be combined with each other and with the elements of a scalar field in the way that vectors can, addition within the group being commutative and associative and multiplication by a scalar being distributive and associative" (OED). This does, however, instantly create a problem: the frequency occurrence pattern of words is a near-perfect Zipfian curve, with a few words highly frequent and the majority of words less and less frequent. Therefore, in English, grammatical words (*the, and, of, to*) are highly frequent, lexical words (*table, teach, tepid, totally*) less so. As a consequence, NLP researchers using vector spaces have devised a nifty, simple strategy to make calculations straightforward (faster and less costly): the vector calculations ignore grammatical words and simply focus on lexical words. In a way, this mimics the spoken production of English, where lexical words carry stress and grammatical ones do not. Furthermore, in discourses, speakers would put extra prominence on those syllables in an utterance that are within lexical words, whereas this extra weight is only given to grammatical words if a situation specifically requires it.

Table 3.2 can serve as a demonstration: Line 1* is a too-complete example, as proper nouns are not preceded by article: slot 1 (s1) and slot 4 (s4) would therefore be marked as zero-article—0. Consequently, Line 2 gives a naturally structured sentence. Line 3 provides the elements that would be fed into the vector computations: only slots s2, s3, s5 and s7. Now, a further simplification can be achieved by cutting out rare words. Neither "Jane" nor "John" are rare, yet they are less frequent than the sum of all names of (1) females and (2) males. Thus, the sentence can be reformulated as in Line 4, resulting into the four lexical units of line 5.[20] Erk and Padó (2008) have refined the original approach with their *structured vector space model* that takes into account word positions—i.e. whether they are at the start, middle or end of a clause; text or paragraph initial, etc.—what they refer to as "preferences for words' argument positions".[21]

How Vector Space Models are working in detail can be found explained in various places. The MLWIKI page by Alexey Grigorev is extremely useful in this case.[22] At a far more technically advanced level, Stephen Clark's "Vector Space Models of lexical meaning" (2015) gives an in-depth description.

If a machine is able to understand, it is also able to reformulate input in order to speed up providing the most likely required output. A patent filed by Amit Singhal and his colleagues, Google engineers, in 2011

Table 3.2 From full sentence to surface forms

	s1	s2	s3	s4	s5	s6	s7
1*	THE	JANE	CALLS	THE	JOHN	A	WOMAN
2		JANE	CALLS		JOHN	A	WOMAN
3		JANE	CALLS		JOHN		WOMAN
4		FEMALE	CALLS		MALE	A	WOMAN
5		FEMALE	CALLS		MALE		WOMAN
	0	NP_1	VP	0	NP_2	Art/0	NP_3

shows how vector spaces can be employed to reword search queries so that the system becomes more accurate in providing the required search result (Fig. 3.8).

The relevant section of the patent filed states "A semantic concept vector may be built by a query processing component, based on the set of N documents that form the query context"—so relevant items in the query will be translated into a vector space model and the query will therefore not be based on the wording created by the human input provider: the query is an automated, artificially created mathematical model that interprets the human input in a way that aims to find the most exact match.

3.5.3 *Language Modelling:* **Long Short-Term Memory** *(LSTM)* *and the* **Recurrent Neural Network** *(RNN)*

This section describes the most up-to-date research into the basic mechanics to deal with source material (corpora of texts) and how these are being used to train the machine to process language input. It demonstrates how the work of Ross Quillian becomes less relevant—though it

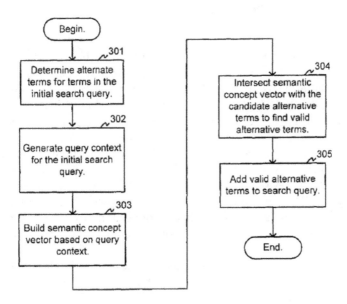

Fig. 3.8 Drawing 3 from Patent No.: US 8,055,669 B1 (Singhal et al., 2011)

is still echoed in current developments and his ideas certainly provided a solid stepping stone to get there. Yet, as the development and commercial (as well as non-commercial, in particular in the military) exploitation of the technology become ever-more poignant, the classical concepts vanish into the background. Computing vectors for complex entities that consists of x amount of separate documents, numbering a total of millions, billions or trillions of words, provides the opportunity to combine the "brute force approach" with the smart applications when it comes to statistics-based evaluation and distribution modelling. Therefore, purely numerical applications allow the highly scientific application for something seen as inherently human and thus bound within the fields of the arts and humanities: language. Vector Space models and statistics now provide a platform to turn "bags of words" back into language communication. One, they allow machines to be trained, and two (once they are comprehenders), their usage can be applied. Training splits into two parts—exposure to material and then ever-more efficient methods created in order to be able to facilitate the parsing of input. Here, the focus will be on only two applications: the first is spoken language understanding,[23] and the second is translation from a source language into a target language. Hirschberg and Manning (2015) gave a concise review of the state of the science of Natural Language Processing in the journal *Science*.

When it comes to training understanders in the twenty-first century, where data are available in large amounts and where highly complex computing tasks are feasible, yet models to decrease the computing time needed remain highly sought after, we have to familiarise ourselves with two concepts: the so-called *Long short-term memory* (LSTM) and the *Recurrent Neural Network (RNN)*. The *Long short-term memory* (LSTM) was first proposed back in 1997 by Sepp Hochreiter and Jürgen Schmidhuber. This provided a hugely refined activation model—though it needed to be revised and tweaked over two decades to find successful applications. They introduce their system as follows: "In principle, recurrent networks can use their feedback connections to store representations of recent inputs in the form of activations (short-term memory embodied by slowly changing weights). This is potentially significant for many applications, including speech processing ..." (Hochreiter and Schmidhuber 1997: 1735). When it comes to RNN, members of the Google Deep mind team describe it as follows:

> Recurrent neural networks (RNNs) stand out from other machine learning methods for their ability to learn and carry out complicated transformations of data over extended periods of time. Moreover, it is known that RNNs are Turing-Complete and therefore have the capacity to simulate arbitrary procedures, if properly wired. (Graves et al. 2014)

The authors further describe that RNNs can be best understood as a digital version of the human "working memory"—the way psychology explains the "performance of tasks involving the short-term manipulation of information". Making reference to the work of Miller (1956), who described how information appears to be stored in "chunks" (see Chapter 4), they describe how technical solutions can overcome and seriously expand the constraints the human working memory has. Both these systems are then used to train machines to understand a language (or, indeed, languages), by employing *language modelling (LM)*. This concept is described by Jozefowicz et al. (2016) describe prior models and describe LM as follows:

> Often (although not always) training better language models improves the underlying metrics of the downstream task (such as word error rate for speech recognition, or BLEU score for translation), which makes the task of training better LMs valuable by itself. Further, when trained on vast amounts of data, language models compactly extract knowledge encoded in the training data. For example, when trained on movie subtitles, these language models are able to generate basic answers to questions about object colors, facts about people, etc. (Jozefowicz et al. 2016)

This, in itself, is quite revolutionary: instead of having human agency gives the machine a grammatical system, the training data provide the blueprint for the machine to discover repeat patterns which provide the model construct it is going to work from. The basis of this can be found in the work of and Mikolov et al. (2010, 2011, 2012)[24] who, over the last decade, have developed the awkwardly named *Recurrent Neural Network based Language Model* (RNN LM) which has subsequently become the model for speech processing software. Mikolov et al. start from the premise that statistical language models have outperformed linguistic language models in real-world applications and they have, thus, become the focus of all recent developments in the field. As a consequence, "[t]he main power of neural network based language models seems to be in their simplicity: almost the same model can be used for prediction of many types of signals, not just language. These models [implicitly] perform clustering of words in low-dimensional space" (Mikolov et al. 2011: 5528). Using such models of predictions has been shown to be robust. Prediction based on this compact representation of words is then more robust. Still, the systems developed until that point focussed on a rather narrow range of neighbouring words: typically, the first two nearest items, as processing longer strings, would have been, in computing terms, a lot more costly. In other words, deeper networks could have been taken into consideration, yet that would require more advanced and higher processor capacity and also more time. The model Mikolov and his collaborators have developed "inserts" a short-term memory function which is not as costly yet as effective (as a number of tests have demonstrated):

> The recurrent neural network based language model provides further generalization: instead of considering just several preceding words, neurons with input from recurrent connections are assumed to represent short term memory. The model learns itself from the data how to represent memory. While shallow feedforward neural networks (those with just one hidden layer) can only cluster similar words, recurrent neural network (which can be considered as a deep architecture) can perform clustering of similar histories. (Mikolov et al. 2011: 5528)

Furthermore, the authors suggest that training should take place not by using one large, unwieldy network, but several small networks which are then combined. Another path chosen to make the system run more efficiently is the approach to rare words/infrequent words, which have been merged into one single token. As a result, they claim that "RNN LM is probably the simplest language model today. And very likely also the most intelligent. (...) This work provides clear connection between machine learning, data compression and language modelling" (Mikolov et al. 2010). One might say that this is a huge claim to make—yet the number of views and citations the *Recurrent Neural Network Model* literature received reflects its impact and the model has been adopted for a number of applications since. Despite all this, there are limitations. Most prominently, Jozefowicz et al. (2016) say that the RNN model has been mainly tested on relatively small-scale source corpora.

Given that access to training material in excess of a billion words was, at the time of writing, relatively easy to obtain, a further permutation of the language modelling systems was required. The model seen as the latest development is the so-called *Long short-term memory* (LSTM) as described by Jozefowicz et al. (2016)—an artificial neural network architecture that supports machine learning. As it is recurrent, it allows data to flow both forwards and backwards within the network. As Manning (2017) points out, "The LSTM gates all operations so stuff can be forgotten/ignored rather than it all being crammed on top of everything else". Thus, the LSTM is well-suited to learn from experience to classify, process and predict time series given time lags of unknown size and bound between important events. As a result, the ability to predict—say how to complete an utterance only started—has been found to be higher than early models allowed.[25] The team demonstrates that the size of training data provides unequalled advantages. Moreover, this approach presents a breakthrough with regard to the so-called *tail-words*[26]: rare or infrequent words show that the LSTM model performs even better than all preceding language modelling approaches. This system performs more successful overall regardless of what the words or word combinations are; in particular, it is a lot better with regard to *rare words* than the (computationally expensive) 5-word-string n-gram models. Consequently, the authors concluded that this "suggest[s] that LSTM LMs may fare even better for languages or data sets where the number of rare words is larger than traditional N-gram models" (Jozefowicz et al. 2016). Post-training, the researchers required validation by looking at a random sample of complex sentences that the system was able to generate. While undoubtedly of exceedingly high quality, they still show some minor errors. Two of which are shown below:

> It is now known that coffee and cacao products can do no harm on the body .< S > Yuri zhirkov was in attendance at the Stamford Bridge at the start of the second half but neither Drogba nor Malouda was able to push on through the Barcelona defence .

Endearingly, the machine happens to make mistakes that are not uncommon for learners of English as a foreign language—for example preposition phrases (*do no harm on* rather than *do no harm to*) or the misplaced definite article which would be correct for *attendance at the bridge* yet, as *Stamford Bridge* is a proper noun, no preceding article is expected. Yet even good systems can be improved. Damavandi et al. (2016) point out that n-gram LMs still have the advantage of scalability—in particular when the training data reach beyond several billions of words. Also, in speech recognition, the system typically deals with short utterances—something where n-gram-based language models excel when compared to LSTMs. These engineers have therefore created a speech recognition system that they call NN-grams, which uses the scalability and capacity to memorise which is typical of n-gram language models. It does, moreover, retain the qualities of neural networks, in particular, the ability to generalise.

3.5.4   *Language Models and Speech Recognition*

Speech recognition systems present a further problem, namely that certain areas of the English language have a very different representation of the same thing when a written form and a spoken form are compared. This becomes quite obvious when a highly frequent area of speech is focussed upon: numerals. Numbers are being used for a wide variety of items: time, day and date; money; house numbers and numbers of floors or flats; classification systems, and so on. Yet there are a variety of options available for a speaker to read out a number seen in written form—these might change due to register, circumstances or idiosyncrasies. Vasserman et al. (2015) give this example:

> First, there is ambiguity with respect to segmentation:
> For example, "forty two dollars and thirty cents" could be transcribed as "$42.30" or "40 $2.30" or "$42 and 30¢", etc.
> Second, there is ambiguity with respect to semantics:
> The words "eleven thirty" could be a time "11:30", a house number "1130" or they can be kept in the verbal domain as "eleven thirty".

They use an LSMT-based model. Above, we have seen how Erk and Pado refined their LM by including word position. The system created by Lucy Vasserman and her colleagues appears to be a speech-recognition system that provides a clear link to the semantic networks proposed by Quillian and his followers: "a method for training context-dependent class-based language models to improve recognition of non-lexical vocabulary items. Using a contextual sequence labelling model to identify class instances in training data mitigates the common problem of context-independent class labelling" (Vasserman et al. 2015). By "non-lexical", they mean items like phone numbers (a number sequence that will occur only once). We see a link to the semantic web in the strong focus on the "contextual", though critics may argue that this model stands and falls with the training data it has. If fully trained on US data, it might work sufficiently well in Britain—yet conventions differ (even on a smaller geographical scale). Both machine-reading tools and speech-recognition tools will be judged by their ability to understand input and their level of comprehension is usually tested through posing queries.

In fact, it is these LM systems which run inside the likes of Amazon's Alexa, Google Go[27] or SIRI in order to facilitate speech recognition without having to individually train the system with each new user. Earlier versions of Google Go—which was launched in 2013 demonstrate the "thinking progress" as a voice requests information. This can be seen on the *Searchengineland* website (last accessed 11/2017):

https://searchengineland.com/googles-impressive-conversational-search-goes-live-on-chrome-160445

In the author's experience,[28] Google Go tends to outperform SIRI (even on IOS 11.3). Both systems allow follow-on questions: they have dialogue capabilities (see below). In fact, where the system needs to "think", the words change in real time in front of the users' eyes. Thus it was observed that in the query "which writer proposes this view" the term "writer" changed to "raita" and back, then back again (and the query failed to get an answer).

When it comes to speech recognition, there is one further element that should be taken into account. As it has been argued above, speech recognition systems can perform well with an n-gram-based core system. What, however, will happen if the command goes beyond "Please switch on the kitchen lights" / "Who played the xyz song first?" / "How many eggs are in a baker's dozen"?—this becomes the domain of the dialogue machines which not only listen in order to respond directly but can imitate full conversations (thus providing a set-up that make digital personal assistants even more effective). The seminal paper by Hermann et al. (2015) appears to hark back to Quillian's *Teachable Language Comprehender*—their paper is entitled *Teaching Machines to Read and Comprehend*. They look at news texts (Daily Mail—UK; CNN—US) to test various models. They created, first of all, an easily visible baseline:

Maximum Frequency, which "picks the entity most frequently observed in the context document" and a related, subtler set-up, named *Exclusive Frequency* which refers to "the entity most frequently observed in the context **but not observed** in the query" (Hermann et al. 2015: 1693, author's highlights).

This simplest of approaches provides a hit-accuracy (i.e. queries are answered correctly) of between 25.5 and 36.6%. This, however, appears to be disappointingly low. The *frame-semantic network* approach, basing on parsing the text (with the *PropBank* parser), fares little better however: 35–40%. What has been found to work considerably better is the system that looks at text-inherent markers, namely *word-distance* which gave accurate returns in over half of all tests. It is, however, the deep neural network—the LSMT described above—mechanism that provides results of the highest accuracy (up to nearly three out of four answers being correct). Hermann and colleagues have, however, modified the system in a way that works well for textual inputs (but would be difficult to implement for voice-activated machines): they have added an extra layer, in fact two layers. One of these is called the "attentive reader" which they describe as using an attention mechanism at sentence level where it "employs a finer grained token level attention mechanism where the tokens are embedded given their entire future and past context in the input document" (ibid.: 1695). The other is called the "impatient reader" system, which uses a different mechanism, namely by focussing simply on those parts of the text which are most likely to provide the necessary information. This model also has the "ability to reread from the document as each query token is read" (ibid.). It can be seen that the engineers had two types of (human) reader in mind—one paying close attention, the other skimming the text for information, and if no results are forthcoming, there is always the opportunity to go over the same text (or passage) again to seek that piece of information that has eluded the reader the first time around.

Jiwei Li and colleagues (2016) further developed the system. They are highlighting the important fact that, in order to have a fluent conversation, the responder must not only react but must also be able to gauge what the first speaker is aiming to say: in a way, predict the near future. They point out that a straightforward *LSTM sequence-to-sequence (SEQ2SEQ) model* can estimate the maximum likelihood of any next turn—but human beings, they point out respond through giving "inter-resting, diverse, and informative feedback that keeps users engaged" (Li et al. 2016). By contrast, existing LSTM machines can too often resort to saying "I don't know" as a response to any kind of query. While this is the most frequent trigram in spoken British English corpora, it is certainly not the default option for natural speakers! A second problem is the repetition, where a conversation system would get stuck in a loop: thus revealing itself as less than human. Like Hermann and colleagues, Li and his fellow collaborators are inspired by human behaviour. Therefore, the machine has an inbuilt reward system that reinforces preferred patterns (and discourages the patterns seen as pitfalls described above). Thus, the system will be prepared by giving it a training set consisting of 80 million source-target pairs. Amongst other things, it employs a "mutual information score [which] will be used as a reward and back-propagated to the encoder-decoder model, tailoring it to generate sequences with higher rewards" (ibid.). The authors tested the machine by letting two virtual agents talk to each other—which is similar to the work by Mike Lewis et al. (forthcoming) performed recently at *Facebook*. Lewis and his fellow engineers demonstrated in their experiment that two robots can achieve highly proficient negotiation skills (linking in with Li's demand to predict future moves). The experiment became quite a media sensation (in July 2017) as the two chatbots at one point appeared to have developed their own language.[29] Both models have training data sets taken from real-life material (here: transcripts of negotiations), use reinforcement learning and are supervised. Lewis et al.'s model is goal-based, and they found that their system appeared to produce good students who can mimic human traits to a recognisable degree: these goal-based models were found to negotiate harder, and this means that they can deceive ("Deception can be an effective negotiation tactic. We found numerous cases of our models initially feigning interest in a valueless item, only to later "compromise" by conceding it" (ibid.)). Another goal had been achieved, as the researchers saw that their robots were able to produce meaningful novel sentences. This, the last point, makes it hugely interesting in the context of this book. While the machine played, 76% of **all** sentences produced came from the training data. What is interesting though is that nearly a quarter of the utterances within text produced were unique. As Lewis and his colleagues describe it:

> [We] found that the overwhelming majority were fluent English sentences in isolation—showing that the model has learnt a good language model for

the domain (in addition to results that show it uses language effectively to achieve its goals). These results suggest that although neural models are prone to the safer option of repeating sentences from training data, they are capable of generalising when necessary. (Lewis et al., forthcoming)

It is this point that shows how the discussion can close the circle fully: because the training data are so highly (domain) specific, it gives the neural network machine the chance to learn the properties of the language as received per input. As a result (an unintentional result in this case), the machine opts to apply the fundamental ground rules thus learned. *Et voilà*: a machine is born that sounds like a natural language producer, rather than a dumb parrot. In fact, as this book is in its production stage, Google, during its Developer's Conference, unveiled *Google Duplex*, the latest development of their AI-driven voice assistant products. Duplex appears more natural to conversation partners as the typical disfluencies of natural speakers are integrated. The result is "...a new technology for conducting natural conversations to carry out "real world" tasks over the phone. The technology is directed towards completing specific tasks, such as scheduling certain types of appointments." The authors describe the technology as follows: "at the core of Duplex is a recurrent neural network (RNN) designed to cope with these challenges, built using TensorFlow Extended (TFX). To obtain its high precision, we trained Duplex's RNN on a corpus of anonymized phone conversation data". (Leviathan and Matias 2018). The demonstration appears, indeed, disconcertingly human-like, understanding typical parts of a service exchange ("hold on one second") while integrating typical discourse particles and back channelling markers ("Hi, um, I'd like" ... "Mm hmm") in their conversation.[30]

3.6   A Brief Look at Language Modelling
for Translation

The area of machine-based translation is several degrees removed from the key issues of this book. No professional translator sees much merit in the digital competition. Likewise, neither Allan Collins, Ross Quillian's former collaborator, nor Yorick Wilks, the British Computer Scientist and Professor Emeritus of artificial intelligence, believes that even the most cutting-edge systems will be able to replace human beings as translators. Nevertheless, the advances made over the last twenty years are not short from remarkable. Quillian (1969) pointed out that "no human translator will translate a text word-for-word"—yet this is exactly what web-based digital "translation software" seemed to offer the user in the 1990s—often with hilarious results. Yet, while "search engine" has now become synonymous with "Google", so has the area of machine translation for casual use "just Google translate it". The range is vastly expanded: there are many more languages now, and Google can employ cameras (to read and translate text) as well as microphones and speakers (to listen and provide interpretation).

At this point, the work of Chris Manning, who did his BA on mathematics, computer science and linguistics, will be briefly discussed. He received a PhD in linguistics at Stanford in 1994 and returned to teach NLP at Stanford in 1999. Also discussed will be the work of Franz Josef Och, who received his PhD from the *Rheinisch-Westfälischen Technischen Hochschule* (Germany's premier engineering university) in 1998, moved to the USA in that same year and had been Head of Machine Translation at Google where he was the chief architect of *Google Translate*.

Och and Manning use the *statistical machine translation* approach, rather than example-based machine translation. In their 2014 patent, Och, Jahr and Thayer describe machine-based translation approaches. We learn, for example, that as a human translator will need both time and adequate payment in the real world, transferring source material into the target language automatically is seen as an important step. The authors write that "statistical machine translation attempts to identify a most probable translation in a target language given a particular input in a source language. Therefore, when translating a sentence from French to English, statistical machine translation identifies the most probable English sentence given the French sentence" (2014a: 1).

Most commonly, a technique that requires zero supervision, the *Minimum Error Rate Training* (MERT) is applied to set up the machine protocol. The technique was first described by Och (2003). It is a development and shares the basic constituents of Och and Ney's (2002) *alignment template approach*. There, the source was split into comprehensible phrases and these were matched to target language phrases. In a second step, the word order was aligned with the standards of the target language. This and MERT are a move away from just testing for basic statistical criteria like maximum likelihood. According to Och and colleagues, "The MERT technique trains parameters for a linear statistical machine translation model directly. With respect to automatic evaluation metrics, i.e. metrics that do not require human evaluation" (2014a: 1). In theory, any metric can be chosen. In practice, training data will check whether there are errors in individual words, in the word order (position error) and the Bilingual Evaluation Understudy (BLEU) score. The disadvantage of the technique is that the more metrics are chosen, the more cumbersome the system becomes, using more computing time and power—thus, a developer needs to find a compromise which is driven by selecting the most effective metrics. While these techniques are used to train the system in order to achieve more natural-sounding target-language translations, the *distributed machine translation* (DMT) is a particular usage of the *distributed machine processing systems,* which can be used for speech recognition, translation, spell-checking or other automated processes. For one, the distribution ensures that the material for the language model can be scaled up (a figure of eight trillion words and upwards, which is to match a translation model of 200 million words was mentioned in Och et al. 2014b). The patent's authors point out that the n-gram-based language models tend to be more effective if access to n-grams larger than 3-grams exist. Distribution means that existing servers are partitioned, or the material is being distributed between (networked) smaller units thus ensuring a faster retrieval rate. When it comes to translation, the following process is employed: the system needs information as to how often various words, phrases or sets of words occur in the **target language** in order to make a translation more comprehensible. If, for example, the target is English, the training data may present the following information (based on Och et al. 2014b):

(1) (is, the, only, person) -> 9234 occurrences
(2) (is, the, only, person, that) -> 173 occurrences
(3) (is, the, only, person, only, that) -> 1 occurrence

It is logical that the longer string (n-gram) (2) is less frequent than the 4-gram (1). The word order in (3), however, makes it a less obvious choice for a natural-sounding target translation. In other words, the system takes a word or phrase in the source language, determines whether it also occurs in the target language and uses the likelihood of larger chunks occurring in the latter as the point of orientation. This would, however, create specific problems where morphologically poor (i.e. English) languages are being translated into morphologically rich (i.e. Russian, Latin, Finnish) languages as a sequence of words needs to be matched into a morphosyntactic structure that may be no longer than a single item.

While the results for this system are notable, the accuracy of their translations was yet higher in a paper presented by Sutskever et al. (2014), using a deep neural network and LSTM (see Sect. 3.5.3). The drawbacks of these, as Jean et al. (2014) point out, are the limitations in handling large vocabulary as it gets disproportionally complex to train and decode the number of target words. Their solution is to use sampling instead of full data sets—and that was the case even when unknown words were being replaced. A solution for translating highly inflected languages successfully has been proposed by Luong and Manning (2016) who modelled a hybrid approach and tested it on Czech. They describe it as follows: "hybrid systems that translate mostly at the *word* level and consult the *character* components for rare words. [The] character-level recurrent neural networks compute source word representations and recover unknown target words when needed" (ibid., italics in the original).

Finally, fast forward to 2017 and the two systems proposed by Melvin Johnson and his Google Research team and Google Brains' Lukasz Kaiser et al. Johnson and colleagues devised a system to simplify the translation of multiple languages. Up to now, translations have been undertaken strictly in pairs (French–English; German–English, etc.). The Google multilingual translation system is described as simple, economical zero-shot translation. The authors explain that, as Google at the time of writing supported 100 different languages, this sum would need to be squared to provide best possible translations for each single pair. Instead, there is just a single procedure which requires no change to the traditional NMT model architecture. Only an artificial token is added to each input sequence to indicate the required target language, a simple amendment to the data only (cf. Johnson et al. 2016:1). As a result, they describe how a system can be trained for the pairs Portuguese–English, and English–Spanish and a reasonable translation from Portuguese to Spanish can be achieved though that pair had never been separately trained. This approach appears to have never been successfully conducted. Overall results are promising: from many source languages into a single target language, it performs slightly better than single pairs. It is, however, worse from a single source into multiple targets. Nevertheless, for low-resource languages, this approach appears to be the most cost-effective high value machine translation possible.

Lukasz Kaiser et al. (2017) go one step further—their ecosystem attempts to combine multiple sensory inputs in order to "read" them, namely multiple translation tasks, image captioning, speech recognition and English parsing. Similar to their colleagues' approach, they combine input sources in order to maximise output efficiency, rather than running a number of systems in parallel. This, in a way, has technology mimicking the human. Things can be processed better and faster if there are multiple sensory stimuli: knowledge of one field helps understanding another better. The same is true for machines: "multi-modal learning has been shown to improve learned representations in the unsupervised setting and when used as a priori known unrelated tasks" (Kaiser et al. 2017: 1f.). Building blocks from different domains are being combined by creating subnetworks so that the input can then be converted into the representation space which covers all perception areas. Kaiser et al. call these *modality nets* as they are specific to each modality. Also, there is only one subnetwork per modality, so not to limit the performance. "For example, all translation tasks share the same modality-net (and vocabulary), no matter for which language pair. This encourages generalisation across tasks and allows to add new tasks on the fly" (Kaiser et al. 2017: 2).

It must be noted that this multimodal approach is still in its fairly early stages. That notwithstanding, a vista of a highly developed, efficient digital brain becomes apparent where seemingly unrelated areas and tasks help to improve the recall and accuracy in understanding, processing and responding to any kind of input. It is also a more holistic approach, one that should chime positively with educators who see how multiple sensory stimulants support the acquisition process of a learner's minds. This therefore presents a most suitable lead-over into Chapter 4.

NOTES

1. Hoey thought that *Lexical Priming* had been a new departure (personal communication). I show, however, that the basic idea is a development of the notion of bonding worked on by Hoey (1991, 1995).
2. In 2017, Hoey would revisit the issue of bonding and lexical priming in his chapter focussing on cohesion and coherence.
3. My favourite example here is the item *inflationary*. The common usage of the term comes from economics: "Of, pertaining to, characterized by, or involving (monetary) inflation" (OED). However, in the domain of astronomy, the word refers to something rather different: "Designating

(a model of) the universe conceived as having had a brief period of exponential expansion shortly after the big bang, before re-entering the regime of linear expansion described by conventional big-bang theory" (OED draft edition, 1993).

4. The pun, here, is intended.

5. Xiao and McEnery (2006: 124ff) indicate that these two terms are very close in meaning; furthermore, the notion seems to be typical not just of one language but of any language.

6. The MI is being calculated by dividing the observed frequency of the co-occurring word in the defined span for the search string (so-called *node word*), for the 5 to the left, 5 to the right window, by the expected frequency of the co-occurring word in that span and then taking the logarithm to the base 2 of the result.

7. Bill Louw published his seminal paper on semantic prosody in 1993. A key item discussed there is the word *utterly* found in a Larkin poem. According to Louw, *utterly* was a rarely used "adult" word (not found in corpora of children's speech). It also had an overwhelmingly "bad" prosody. Ironically, in about that time (1995) a British margarine was launched with the "quirky" name "Utterly Butterly"—which led to an explosion of things being pre-modified with the adjective "utterly" by, in particular, younger people.

8. For a child of the 1970s like me that is not really that long ago.

9. Cambria and White (2014) also refer to Robert Simmons (1963).

10. This depends very much on the data. In my spoken corpus, there are 535 instances of *bread* and the collocates *shop* and *home* occur three times each.

11. Looking back at Sect. 3.1, it can be spotted that there is a link in the way Tony Berber Sardinha (2017) found that collocations can predict register variation.

12. Norvig (1987) refers to this as "marker strength".

13. It is also the language that changes. So, for MR Quillian, the activation spread from a *token* (*node*) to other nodes; it can be an *trigger* and *nodes,* Mac an tSaoir speaks of *starting nodes* or *instance IDs* and *associated relationships* (*edges*). *Edges* are, amongst computational linguists or NLP researchers, the links between nodes inside a semantic network. The *strength* of the association or link is referred to as *weight*.

14. Readers may remember that such a hierarchical structure had become problematic as well and that it was finally disposed of by Collins and Loftus in favour of a purely spread activation-based set of linkages.

15. Mac an tSaoir (*) uses the term "surface forms" here for "words found in text form"– "synonyms" of heart in this case. The entry for *heart* is based on data as provided by the NCI Metathesaurus (NCIm), a biomedical

terminology database. The URL for the term is given below (last accessed 03/2018): https://ncim.nci.nih.gov/ncimbrowser/pages/concept_details. jsf?dictionary=NCI%20Metathesaurus&code=C0018787&type=properties.

16. Cost is not just a figure of speech here—the computing time and energy needed for this indeed has to be paid in pennies and pounds, especially for high-performance computers. Thanks to K. H. Wieners for pointing this out.

17. Lecture 10 of *Natural Language Processing with Deep Learning CS224N/ Ling284*, Christopher Manning.

18. Peter Norvig, personal communication (email, November 2015).

19. Franz Josef Och and Hermann Ney (2003) give an overview of statistical modelling (with a particular focus on machine translation) with their paper "A Systematic Comparison of Various Statistical Alignment Models".

20. Interestingly, "female calls male woman", though an incomplete clause, can be perfectly well understood: it has the qualities of a (generic) newspaper headline.

21. This appears to echo work done by Michael Hoey and Matthew Brook O'Donnell (first described at PALC 2007) who looked in how far words are *primed* for their position within a text. See "The beginning of something important: Corpus evidence on the text beginnings of hard news stories". *Corpus Linguistics, Computer Tools, and Applications–State of the Art. Bern: Peter Lang* (2008): 189–212.

22. Alexey Grigorev (2017), "Vector Space Models". In MLWIKI, available at http://mlwiki.org/index.php/Vector_Space_Models (last accessed 11/2017).

23. Henderson (2015), Machine Learning for Dialog State Tracking: A Review Gives a Brief Overview of the Recent Developments.

24. Tomas Mikolov has a very helpful site that provides access to various versions of the toolkit: http://www.fit.vutbr.cz/~imikolov/rnnlm/ (last accessed November 2017).

25. "We hope that our encouraging results, which improved the best perplexity of a single model from 51.3 to 30.0 (while reducing the model size considerably), and set a new record with ensembles at 23.7" as the authors write. Within statistical modelling in information theory, a *low* perplexity score indicates a good or high level of being able to predict.

26. This is a reference to the Zipfian distribution, where highly frequent words can be found at the high start of the curve (few words occur with high frequency) whereas the majority of the words are less frequent, all the way to the rare words, which form the tail-end of the curve (a large number of words which are of low frequency).

27. Confusingly, *Google Go* is the name of Google's search assistant (https:// play.google.com/store/apps/details?id=com.google.android.apps.

searchlite&hl=en) as well as the name of a programming language, created by Google engineers in 2009 (https://golang.org).

28. A short video, rather than screenshot, showing how *Google Go* works can be seen here: https://www.youtube.com/watch?v=CyqsUuKaRv4 (last accessed 11/2017).

29. See *The Register* for a level-headed assessment—https://www.theregister.co.uk/2017/08/01/facebook_chatbots_did_not_invent_new_language/ (last accessed 11/2017) or the British newspaper *The Independent* for a more sensationalist take: http://www.independent.co.uk/life-style/gadgets-and-tech/news/facebook-artificial-intelligence-ai-chatbot-new-language-research-openai-google-a7869706.html (last accessed 11/2017).

30. A demonstration and discussion of Google Duplex can be found on the CNET site: https://www.cnet.com/features/google-assistant-duplex-at-io-could-become-the-most-lifelike-ai-voiceassistant-yet/? (last accessed 09/2018)

REFERENCES

Cambria, Erik, and White Bebo. 2014. Jumping NLP Curves: A Review of Natural Language Processing Research. *EEE Computational Intelligence Magazine* 9 (2): 48–57.

Canhasi, Ercan. 2016. GSolver: Artificial Solver of Word Association Game. In *ICT Innovations 2015*, ed. Suzana Loshkovska and Saso Koceski, 49–57. Cham: Springer.

Carroll, Glenn, and Eugene Charniak. 1991. A Probabilistic Analysis of Marker-Passing Techniques for Plan-Recognition. In *Proceedings of the Seventh Conference on Uncertainty in Artificial Intelligence*, August, 69–76. Morgan Kaufmann Publishers Inc.

Charniak, Eugene. 1972. Toward a Model of Children's Story Comprehension. *AI-Tech*, Rep-266. Cambridge, MA: MIT AI Labs.

Charniak, Eugene. 1986. A Neat Theory of Marker Passing. *AAAI*, 584–588.

Charniak, Eugene, and Robert Goldman. 1988. A Logic for Semantic Interpretation. In *Proceedings of the 26th Annual Meeting on Association for Computational Linguistics*, 87–94. Association for Computational Linguistics.

Clark, Stephen. 2015. Vector Space Models of Lexical Meaning. In *Handbook of Contemporary Semantic Theory*, ed. Shalom Lappin and Chris Fox, 493–522. New York: Wiley.

Collins, Allan M., and Elizabeth F. Loftus. 1975. A Spreading-Activation Theory of Semantic Processing. *Psychological Review* 82 (6): 407–428.

Collobert, Ronan, and Jason Weston. 2008. A Unified Architecture for Natural Language Processing: Deep Neural Networks with Multitask Learning. In

Proceedings of the 25th International Conference on Machine Learning, 160–167. Helsinki, Finland: ACM.

Damavandi, Babak, Shankar Kumar, Noam Shazeer, and Antoine Bruguier. 2016. NN-Grams: Unifying Neural Network and N-Gram Language Models for Speech Recognition. *arXiv preprint* arXiv:1606.07470.

Das, Dipanjan, Desai Chen, André F.T. Martins, Nathan Schneider, and Noah A. Smith. 2014. Frame-Semantic Parsing. *Computational Linguistics* 40 (1): 9–56.

Erk, Katrin, and Sebastian Padó. 2008. A Structured Vector Space Model for Word Meaning in Context. In *Proceedings of the Conference on Empirical Methods in Natural Language Processing*, 897–906. Association for Computational Linguistics.

Graves, Alex, Greg Wayne, and Ivo Danihelka. 2014. Neural Turing Machines. *arXiv preprint* arXiv:1410.5401.

Harabagiu, Sanda M., and Dan I. Moldovan. 1997. Parallel Inference on a Linguistic Knowledge Base. In *Parallel Processing Symposium, 1997. Proceedings, 11th International*, 204–208. IEEE.

Harrington, Brian. 2010. A Semantic Network Approach to Measuring Relatedness. In *Proceedings of the 23rd International Conference on Computational Linguistics: Posters*, 356–364.

Henderson, Matthew. 2015. Machine Learning for Dialog State Tracking: A Review. *Machine Learning in Spoken Language Processing Workshop*. https://static.googleusercontent.com/media/research.google.com/en//pubs/archive/44018.pdf. Last Accessed 11/2017.

Hermann, Karl Moritz, Tomas Kocisky, Edward Grefenstette, Lasse Espeholt, Will Kay, Mustafa Suleyman, and Phil Blunsom. 2015. Teaching Machines to Read and Comprehend. *Advances in Neural Information Processing Systems*, 1693–1701.

Hirschberg, Julia, and Christopher D. Manning. 2015. Advances in Natural Language Processing. *Science* 349 (6245): 261–266.

Hobbs, Jerry R., Mark Stickel, Paul Martin, and Douglas Edwards. 1988. Interpretation as Abduction. In *Proceedings of the 26th Annual Meeting on Association for Computational Linguistics*, 95–103. Association for Computational Linguistics.

Hochreiter, Sepp, and Jürgen Schmidhuber. 1997. Long Short-Term Memory. *Neural Computation* 9 (8): 1735–1780.

Hoey, Michael. 1991. *Patterns of Lexis in Text*. Oxford: Oxford University Press.

Hoey, Michael. 1995. The Lexical Nature of Intertextuality: A Preliminary Study. In *Organization in Discourse: Proceedings from the Turku Conference*, ed. B. Warvik, S. Tanskanen, and R. Hiltunen, 73–94. Anglicana Turkuensia 14.

Hoey, Michael. 2005. *Lexical Priming: A New Theory of Words and Language*. London: Routledge.

Hoey, Michael. 2008. Lexical Priming and Literary Creativity. In *Text, Discourse and Corpora*, ed. M. Hoey, M. Mahlberg, M. Stubbs, and W. Teubert, 7–30. London: Continuum.

Hoey, Michael. 2017. Cohesion and Coherence in a Content-Specific Corpus. In *Lexical Priming: Applications and Advances*, ed. M. Pace-Sigge and K. J. Patterson, 3–40. Amsterdam: John Benjamins.

Jantunen, Jarmo Harri. 2017. Lexical and Morphological Priming. In *Lexical Priming: Applications and Advances*, ed. M. Pace-Sigge and K. J. Patterson, 253–272. Amsterdam: John Benjamins.

Jantunen, Jarmo Harri, and Sisko Brunni. 2013. Morphology, Lexical Priming and Second Language Acquisition: A Corpus-Study on Learner Finnish. In *Twenty Years of Learner Corpus Research: Looking Back, Moving Ahead*, ed. Sylviane Granger, Gaëtanelle Gilquin, and Fanny Meunier, pp. 235–245. Louvain-la-Neuve: Presses universitaires de Louvain.

Jean, Sébastien, Kyunghyun Cho, Roland Memisevic, and Yoshua Bengio. 2014. On Using Very Large Target Vocabulary for Neural Machine Translation. *arXiv preprint* arXiv:1412.2007.

Johnson, Melvin, M. Schuster, Q.V. Le, M. Krikun, Y. Wu, Z. Chen, N. Thorat, F. Viégas, M. Wattenberg, G. Corrado, and M. Hughes. 2016. Googles Multilingual Neural Machine Translation System: Enabling Zero-Shot Translation. *arXiv preprint* arXiv:1611.04558.

Jozefowicz, Rafal, Oriol Vinyals, Mike Schuster, Noam Shazeer, and Yonghui Wu. 2016. Exploring the Limits of Language Modeling. *arXiv preprint* arXiv:1602.02410.

Kaiser, Lukasz, Aidan N. Gomez, Noam Shazeer, Ashish Vaswani, Niki Parmar, Llion Jones, and Jakob Uszkoreit. 2017. One Model to Learn Them All. *arXiv preprint* arXiv:1706.05137.

Lehmann, Fritz. 1992. Semantic Networks. *Computers & Mathematics with Applications* 23 (2–5): 1–50.

Leviathan, Yaniv and Matias, Yossi. 2018. Google Duplex: An AI System for Accomplishing Real World Tasks Over the Phone. *Google AI Blog*. https://ai. googleblog.com/2018/05/duplex-ai-system-for-natural-conversation.html. Last Accessed 09/2018.

Lewis, Mike, Denis Yarats, Yann N. Dauphin, Devi Parikh, and Dhruv Batra. 2018, Forthcoming. Deal or No Deal? End-to-End Learning for Negotiation Dialogues. arXiv:1706.05125.

Li, Jiwei, Will Monroe, Alan Ritter, Michel Galley, Jianfeng Gao, and Dan Jurafsky. 2016. Deep Reinforcement Learning for Dialogue Generation. *arXiv preprint* arXiv:1606.01541.

Louw, Bill. 1993. Irony in the Text or Insincerity in the Writer? The Diagnostic Potential of Semantic Prosodies. In *Text and Technology*, ed. M. Baker, G. Francis, and E. Tognini-Bonelli, 157–176. Amsterdam: Benjamins.

Luong, Minh-Thang, and Christopher D. Manning. 2016. Achieving Open Vocabulary Neural Machine Translation with Hybrid Word-Character Models. *arXiv preprint* arXiv:1604.00788.

Mac an tSaoir, Ronan. 2014. Using Spreading Activation to Evaluate and Improve Ontologies. *COLING*, 2237–2248.

Manin, Yuri I., and Matilde Marcolli. 2016. Semantic Spaces. *Mathematics in Computer Science* 10 (4): 459–477.

Manning, Chris (with Richard Socher). 2017. Natural Language Processing with Deep Learning CS224N/Ling284. Lecture 11. Stanford University.

Mikolov, Tomáš, Martin Karafiát, Lukas Burget, Jan Cernocký, and Sanjeev Khudanpur. 2010. Recurrent Neural Network Based Language Model. *Interspeech* 2: 3–10.

Mikolov, Tomáš, Stefan Kombrink, Lukáš Burget, Jan Černocký, and Sanjeev Khudanpur. 2011. Extensions of Recurrent Neural Network Language Model. *Acoustics, Speech and Signal Processing (ICASSP), 2011 IEEE International Conference on*, 5528–5531.

Mikolov, Tomas, and Geoffrey Zweig. 2012. Context Dependent Recurrent Neural Network Language Model. *Microsoft Research Technical Report MSR-TR-2012-92*, 234–239.

Mikolov, Tomas, Kai Chen, Greg Corrado, and Jeffrey Dean. 2013. Efficient Estimation of Word Representations in Vector Space. *arXiv preprint* arXiv:1301.3781.

Miller, George A. 1956. The Magical Number Seven, Plus or Minus Two: Some Limits on Our Capacity for Processing Information. *Psychological Review*, 63 (2): 81–97.

Neely, James H. 1976. Semantic Priming and Retrieval from Lexical Memory: Evidence for Facilitatory and Inhibitory Processes. *Memory and Cognition* 4 (5): 648–654.

Noordman-Vonk, Wietske. 1979. *Retrieval from Semantic Memory*. Berlin, Heidelberg: Springer.

Norvig, P. 1983. Frame Activated Inferences in a Story Understanding Program. *International Joint Conference on Artificial Intelligence (IJCAI)*, 624–626.

Norvig, P. 1987. *A Unified Theory of Inference for Text Understanding*. PhD thesis, University of California, Berkeley.

Norvig, P. 1989a. Marker Passing as a Weak Method for Text Inferencing. *Cognitive Science* 13 (4): 569–620.

Norvig, P. 1989b. Building a Large Lexicon with Lexical Network Theory. In *Proceedings of the IJCAI Workshop on Lexical Acquisition*, 1–12.

Norvig, P. 1992. Story Analysis. In *Encyclopedia of AI*, ed. Stuart Shapiro. New Jersey: Wiley.

Norvig, P. 2011. On Chomsky and the Two Cultures of Statistical Learning. On-Line Essay in Response to Chomskys Remarks. Available from http://norvig.com/chomsky.html. Last Accessed 11/2017.

Och, Franz Josef. 2003. Minimum Error Rate Training in Statistical Machine Translation. In *Proceedings of the 41st Annual Meeting on Association for Computational Linguistics*, vol. 1, 160–167. Association for Computational Linguistics.

Och, Franz Josef, and Hermann Ney. 2002. Discriminative Training and Maximum Entropy Models for Statistical Machine Translation. In *Proceedings of the 40th Annual Meeting of the Association for Computational Linguistics (ACL)*, Philadelphia, PA.

Och, Franz Josef, and Hermann Ney. 2003. A Systematic Comparison of Various Statistical Alignment Models. *Computational Linguistics* 29: 19–51.

Och, Franz Josef, Michael E. Jahr, and Ignacio E. Thayer. 2014a. Minimum Error Rate Training with a Large Number of Features for Machine Learning. U.S. Patent 8,645,119.

Och, F.J., J. Dean, T. Brants, A.M. Franz, J. Ponte, P. Xu, S.M. Teh, J. Chin, I.E. Thayer, A. Carver, and D. Rosart. 2014b. Encoding and Adaptive, Scalable Accessing of Distributed Models. U.S. Patent 8,738,357.

Pace-Sigge, Michael. 2013. *Lexical Priming in Spoken English Usage*. Houndmills: Palgrave Macmillan.

Pace-Sigge, Michael, and Katie J. Patterson. 2017. *Lexical Priming: Applications and Advances*. Amsterdam: John Benjamins.

Patterson, Katie J. 2016. The Analysis of Metaphor: To What Extent Can the Theory of Lexical Priming Help Our Understanding of Metaphor Usage and Comprehension? *Journal of Psycholinguistic Research* 45 (2): 237–258.

Patterson, Katie J. 2018. *Understanding Metaphor through Corpora: A Case Study of Metaphors in Nineteenth Century Writing*. New York: Routledge.

Quillian, M. Ross. 1966. Semantic Memory. Unpublished Doctoral Dissertation, Carnegie Institute of Technology (Reprinted in Part in M. Minsky (ed.), *Semantic Information Processing*. Cambridge: MIT Press, 1968).

Quillian, M. Ross. 1969. The Teachable Language Comprehender: A Simulation Program and Theory of Language. *Computational Linguistics* 12 (8) (August): 459–476.

Sardinha, Tony Berber. 2017. Lexical Priming and Register Variation. In *Lexical Priming: Applications and Advances*, ed. M. Pace-Sigge and K. J. Patterson, 189–230. Amsterdam: John Benjamins.

Shastri, Lokendra. 1992. Structured Connectionist Networks of Semantic Networks. *Computers & Mathematics with Applications* 23 (2–5): 293–328.

Simmons, Robert. 1963. Synthetic Language Behaviour. *Data Processing Manager* 5 (12): 11–18.

Sinclair, John M. 1987. The Nature of the Evidence. In *Looking Up*, ed. J. Sinclair, 150–159. London: Collins.

Sinclair, John M. 1991. *Corpus, Concordance, Collocation*. Oxford: Oxford University Press.

Singhal, Amit, Mehran Sahami, John Lamping, Marcin Kaszkiel, and Monika H. Henzinger. Google Inc. 2011. Search Queries Improved Based on Query Semantic Information. U.S. Patent 8,055,669.

Sowa, John F. 1987. Semantic Networks. In *Encyclopedia of Artificial Intelligence*, ed. Stuart C. Shapiro. London: Wiley.

Steyvers, Mark, and Joshua B. Tenenbaum. 2005. The Large-Scale Structure of Semantic Networks: Statistical Analyses and a Model of Semantic Growth. *Cognitive Science* 29 (1): 41–78.

Stubbs, Michael. 1995. Collocations and Cultural Connotations of Common Words. *Linguistics and Education* 7 (4): 379–390.

Sutskever, Ilya, Oriol Vinyals, and Quoc V. Le. 2014. Sequence to Sequence Learning with Neural Networks. In *Advances in Neural Information Processing Systems*, 3104–3112.

Szymanski, Julian, and Duch Włodzisław. 2012. Annotating Words Using WordNet Semantic Glosses. In *International Conference on Neural Information Processing (ICONIP) 2012*, ed. Julian Szymański and Włodzisław Duch, 180–187. Part IV, LNCS 7666.

Teufl, Peter, and Stefan Kraxberger. 2011. Extracting Semantic Knowledge from Twitter. In *Electronic Participation*, 48–59.

Titchener, Edward B. 1922. A Note on Wundts Doctrine of Creative Synthesis. *The American Journal of Psychology* 33 (3): 351–360.

Touretzky, David. 1986. *The Mathematics of Inheritance Systems*. London: Pitman Publishing.

Vasserman, Lucy, Vlad Schogol, and Keith Hall. 2015. Sequence-Based Class Tagging for Robust Transcription in ASR. In *Sixteenth Annual Conference of the International Speech Communication Association*.

Whitsitt, Sam. 2005. A Critique of the Concept of Semantic Prosody. *International Journal of Corpus Linguistics* 10 (3): 283–305.

Wilensky, Robert. 1978. Understanding Goal Based Stories. *Yale University Computer Science Research Report*, New Haven, CT.

Wilensky, Robert. 1982. *Story Points, Strategies for Natural Language Processing*. New York: Erlbaum.

Wilensky, Robert. 1983. Memory and Inference. In *International Joint Conference on Artificial Intelligence (IJCAI)*, 402–404.

Wu, Dekai 1989. A Probabilistic Approach to Marker Propagation. In *International Joint Conference on Artificial Intelligence (IJCAI)*, 574–582.

Wundt, Wilhelm Max. 1862. *Beiträge zur Theorie der Sinneswahrnehmung*. Leipzig und Heidelberg: Wintersche Verlagsbuchhandlung.

Xiao, Richard. n.d. Corpus Linguistics: The Basics. Making Statistical Claims (PPT). www.lancaster.ac.uk/fass/projects/corpus/ZJU/xpresentations/session%205.ppt. Last Accessed 10/2017.

Xioa, Richard, and Tony McEnery. 2006. Collocation, Semantic Prosody, and Near Synonymy: A Cross-Linguistic Perspective. *Applied Linguistics* 27 (1): 103–129.

Yu, Yeong-Ho, and Robert F. Simmons. 1988. Constrained Marker Passing. Artificial Intelligence Laboratory, University of Texas at Austin.

CHAPTER 4

Take Home Messages for Linguists and Artificial Intelligence Designers

Abstract When looking at AI engineers on the one hand and linguists on the other, it is easy to assume that they have nothing in common. However, rather than being like two tribes that are living and working in parallel, these groups of researchers have a number of common roots, as this chapter will describe. This chapter will explore developments in areas of linguistic research which, so far, have not been seen in AI applications. Conversely, that a large number of digital tools can understand, process and even produce language reasonably well by now, can give linguists a vital input into the direction of their research: clearly, certain models work very well when language is described, others, however, less well.

Keywords Norvig · Manning · Pragmatics · Hapax legomena
Discourse analysis

4.1   INTRODUCTION

This chapter is divided into three distinct parts. First of all, the reader will be introduced to either the background or strong interest in linguistic studies and phenomena amongst prominent figures in the current Artificial intelligence (AI) development community. Next, a brief overview of areas in language research that have not, so far, found much application in contemporary AI will be given: thus, some of the issues

M. Pace-Sigge, *Spreading Activation,*
Lexical Priming and the Semantic Web,
https://doi.org/10.1007/978-3-319-90719-2_4

and key points where AI developers can directly learn from active linguists will be highlighted. The final section, 4.4, acts as a summing-up of the different approaches to process language and offers a proposal in what way this can be viewed as a way to understand language as such.

4.2   AI Developers—Where They Come from

4.2.1   Introduction

In the course of this book, the reader might have seen the computational specialists on the one side—starting with Turing and Minsky—and all the way to Norvig, Manning and Och and finally whole teams of engineers. On the other side are the corpus linguists like Sinclair, Louw and Hoey. Somewhere in the middle are those who focus on the psychological processes: G. A. Miller, Meyer and Schvaneveldt, Collins and Loftus. For me, it is Ross Quillian who provided the linking element, connecting the ideas of human neural connections in the mind with concepts of how a machine could run along the same principles. Out of this, the idea of the *semantic net,* proposed by Quillian in 1969, has developed a concept both taken up amongst linguistics and computational engineering.[1] Out of this, there is the process of *spreading activation* where connections between words spring from *primed nodes* (the idea taken up by Meyer and Schvaneveldt and then applied by Hoey to explain the phenomena uncovered by corpus linguists). This system has also been applied to create text-understanding machines in a recognisable form to this day.

The question is, however, whether we are really dealing with two tribes that are living and working in parallel—or are these groups of researchers bound together by more than just the common use of corpora?

To go right back to the beginning, the idea of "corpora" is nothing new: its roots lie in bible exegesis, which dug deep into the origins of the religious texts. After all, the bible is a corpus—a collection of a large variety of texts, physically written down by various people over a long time span. Indeed, the concept of concordancing, putting lines together that have the same target word, emanated out of these studies. In modern day parlance, a corpus is, however, a structured collection of texts, made to be computer-readable and therefore fully analysable with digital tools. The first of these modern corpora was Henry Kučera's *Brown Corpus of Standard American English* (1963–1964) which was a carefully assembled collection of written texts of a large variety of genres, amounting to the then huge number of one million words. Between 1970 and 1977, the British English equivalent, the Lancaster Oslo Bergen (LOB)—after the universities involved in the project) corpus was created. Like its American counterpart, the Lancaster-Oslo-Bergen Corpus contains 500 printed texts of about 2000 words each, or about a million running words in all. The year of publication (1961) and the sampling principles are identical to those of the Brown Corpus, though there were necessarily some differences in text selection. This has to be mentioned, given that today, in 2017, corpora can be created by hoovering data from the web within very small time frames—yet these corpora number several billions of words. Similarly, Quillian describes in the 1960s how his *TLC* can be fed a collection of twenty texts of a particular genre—in effect a small, specialist corpus—while today such collections are automated to a high degree, with machines ordering text genre according to relevant tags. The remaining constant is that both linguists and computational linguists (be they working in *Machine Learning* or *NLP*) focus on human language—a complex entity that must be understood to a certain degree in order to conduct research or create digital applications. Yet, with the clear trend towards complete automation, is there less influence by linguists on the second side to be seen—if there had been any influence at all? In order to answer this, I would like to focus on some of the key figures in AI.

4.2.2 Philosophers of Language, Linguists and AI Engineers

First of all, there is the Austrian-British philosopher Ludwig Wittgenstein, whose thoughts and works suggest the necessary bridge, as he concerned himself with the philosophy of mathematics, the philosophy of mind, as well as the area he is probably best known for, the philosophy of language. Already in 1933, Wittgenstein posed the question "can a machine think?" (cf. Shanker 1987) and while we have not got a full record of all their conversations and discussions, it is clear that he and Turing debated the issue of a "mechanical mind":

> Turing met Wittgenstein, and there is a full record of their 1939 discussions on the foundations of mathematics in Diamond (1976). To the disappointment of many, there is no record of any discussions between them, verbal or written, on the problem of Mind.[2]

Yet, Wittgenstein's influence goes even further, as Stuart Russell and Peter Norvig indicate in their comprehensive book on AI:

> Building on the work of Ludwig Wittgenstein (1889–1951) and Bertrand Russell (1872–1970), (...) Rudolf Carnap (1891–1970), developed the doctrine of logical positivism. Carnap's book The Logical Structure of the World (1928) defined an explicit computational procedure for extracting knowledge from elementary experiences. It was probably the first theory of mind as a computational process. (Russell and Norvig 2005: 7)

Moreover, references to the philosophy of language still crop up when talking to mathematically minded engineers. Indeed, a *Google Search* engineer told Steven Levy that the problem of disambiguating synonyms—a crucial issue in order to get search results right—was fixed "by a breakthrough late in 2002 that utilized Ludwig Wittgenstein's theories on how words are defined by context" (2011: 47).

Similarly, Ross Quillian does not simply make use of Ogden's Dictionary of the English Language. His PhD and research papers reflects a thorough debate concerning the linguistic concepts put forward by Chomsky, Charles Fillmore, Susan Ervin (now Ervin-Tripp), Jerrold J. Katz, George Lakoff and Sidney Lamb. What is interesting here is that Quillian measures linguistic theories against the practice of a language machine. In doing so, he confirms theories, for example with regard to prepositions where he says "[i]t would appear that using prepositions to label intertoken links refines the memory's ability to differentiate these relationships in a way that matches the more differentiated parameter symbols that Fillmore shows a need for" (Quillian 1966: 154). Crucially though, throughout his work it can be seen that Quillian struggles to find a place for Chomsky's conception of language, the *transformational-generative grammar* (TGG). The connectional framework is discussed in detail. While he indicates that the machine does create "transformations" (doing them, rather than describing them), his approach to bend any input of "anomalous" sentence to a "well-formed" one is strikingly different.[3] In fact, the segmentation of a generative grammar seems to founder on the realities of processing language: "while generative grammars are very natural parts of a sentence production mechanism, these same grammars raise immediate problems when one attempts to base a parsing or understanding program on them" (Ibid.: 160). In fact, Quillian is very clear that a listener or reader "must retrace the steps by which a sentence might have been generated in order to understand it" (ibid.: 161). Fundamentally, Chomsky's ideas of language appear to have no real value when it comes to real-world applications. In describing his *Teachable Language Comprehender* (TLC), Quillian writes:

> The relation between TLC, a semantic performance model, and the syntactic "competence" models of transformational linguistics (Chomsky 1965) is not clear. The efforts that have been made so far to attach "semantics" to transformational models seem, to this writer at least, to have achieved little success (Woods 1968, being the most significant attempt.) Correspondingly, TLC so far works with syntax on a relatively local, primitive basis, which has very little if anything new to say to a linguist about syntax. (Quillian 1969: 8)

This, however, is not the only time that criticism of the TGG and its main proponent have been raised (as will be shown below). Chomsky had the option to follow the key tenets proposed by his doctoral supervisor, Zellig Harris. Harris, in a posthumously published article describes how words stand in a relative location to each other that is governed by the rules of probability. In fact, what he writes could have been found in Quillian or Meyer-Schvaneveldt, Neely or Hoey: "for each word there are some words that have positive probability of occurring under or over it, while the other words have zero probability there". Furthermore, as a consequence, this: "The *meaning of a word* is indicated, and *in part created*, by the meanings of the words in respect to which it has higher than average probability" (Harris 2002: 217, author's highlights). Nor is this something entirely new when it comes to Harris' language theories. In fact, it has been pointed out that it is time to reassess his work and see the clear link to what can be found in current AI research. Thus, the NLP specialist Fernando Pereira wrote a paper titled "Formal Grammar and Information Theory – Together again?" where he pushes this idea. Pereira says he is broadly interested in linguistics and cognitive sciences but his PhD (University of Edinburgh, 1982) is in AI and he used to be head of Machine Learning at AT&T Labs. Today (2017), he is Vice President and Research Fellow at Google. Pereira describes that Harris, in 1951 and 1991, had himself "advocated a close alliance between grammatical and information-theoretic principles in the analysis of natural language" (Pereira 2000: 1) and early formal-language theory was indeed a bridge between the sphere of information theory and the field of linguistics. The split, widely recognised, came with the claims made by Chomsky as early as 1957[4] (his dismissal of any possible statistical model for grammaticalness)—about which, later. In 1988, Harris himself described a set of four constraints that bring formal grammar and information theory together:

1. **Partial Order** (which will be ignored here, as it seems to only apply to very simple clauses).
2. **Likelihood**—this translates into collocation, along Firthian lines, in corpus linguistics. Within NLP, it reflects the statistical likelihood of one word of set of words to occur with another—something eventually calculated through vector spaces.
3. **Reduction**—like an extended form of (1) but able to cover complex clauses. Again, within corpus linguistics, this appears close to Sinclair's and Hoey's definition of *colligation*—the grammatical category, function and nesting a word would be found in. Within NLP, this is addressed by long n-grams and, as shown above, LSTMs are a very resourceful way to mimic grammatical structures.
4. **Linearisation** (which Harris did not describe in much detail. It might be that he meant to indicate that spoken language production is purely linear, while a written text can be recursive, amongst other things).

Most notability, Harris' model, described as *dependency* and *selection,* is very close to what Hoey (2005) describes as lexical priming. Co-selections are made based on (observable) co-occurrence in words and this, in turn, creates a structure (or: "creates a grammar"). Unlike Chomsky's approach which is very narrowly sentence-based, Harris' model "is lexicalized in the sense that all postulated relationships are between the words in (precursors for) sentences" (Pereira 2000: 8). Yet, even more crucially (and yet more divergent from Chomsky) Harris' models "factor the sentence generation process into a sequence of conditionally independent events (…) That is, the models are in effect lexically-based stochastic generative grammars" (ibid.). Pereira does sound a note of warning however describing how both *formal grammar* and simplistic information theory, giving only intrinsic values to texts (or utterances or signals).[5] This was one of the major criticisms Peter Norvig raised against Quillian's approach (3.2). Nevertheless, *inference*—which can be fully based on statistical calculations—is one approach to infer meaning and the aim of what a source tries to convey.

While Manning (2002) indicates that Chomsky cannot be fully dismissed, his defence, in the end, appears to be little more than a reference to the *competence* vs. *performance* discussion. Yorick Wilks (1985) has raised the accusation that "the real problem with Chomsky's theories is that he has progressively cut himself off from all the areas of intellectual endeavor with the ability to test claims". Yet, while Chomsky has picked many a fight, using arguments which seem almost impossible to contradict, it was Peter Norvig who took up the challenge in 2011 (published in 2012), in direct response to Chomsky deriding the efforts of researchers of machine learning and questioning statistical modelling. The paper actually addresses a range of points. For example, Norvig agrees that a Markov model of word probabilities cannot model all language—only to then highlight that Chomsky appears to dismiss **all** probabilistic models simply because one particular model, now over 50 years old, has clear shortcomings in undertaking such a task. Indeed, any time language is being processed, the receiver has to decide—what the speaker or writer is **likely** to mean:

> Many phenomena in science are stochastic, and the simplest model of them is a probabilistic model; I believe language is such a phenomenon and therefore that probabilistic models are our best tool for representing facts about language, for algorithmically processing language, and for understanding how humans process language. (Norvig 2011)

This "belief" does not come out of nowhere. Norvig describes that he tried to "make language models work using logical rules" until he switched to the probabilistic model. Famously, he never looked back. One of the claims Chomsky made was that probabilistic models "had limited success in some application errors". While the definition of "success" might be debatable, this is what Peter Norvig lists to counter it:

- Search engines
- Speech recognition
- Machine translation

In *Syntactic Structures,* Chomsky introduces a now-famous example that is another criticism of finite-state probabilistic models:

Neither (a) 'colorless green ideas sleep furiously' nor (b) 'furiously sleep ideas green colorless', nor *any of their parts*, has ever occurred in the past linguistic experience of an English speaker. But (a) is grammatical, while (b) is not.

Chomsky appears to be correct that neither sentence appeared in the published literature before 1955. I'm not sure what he meant by "any of their parts," but certainly every two-word part had occurred, for example:

• "It is neutral green, **colorless green**, like the glaucous water lying in a cellar." The Paris we remember, Elisabeth Finley Thomas (1942).
• "To specify those **green ideas** is hardly necessary, but you may observe Mr. [D. H.] Lawrence in the role of the satiated aesthete." The New Republic: Volume 29 p. 184, William White (1922).
• "**Ideas sleep** in books." Current Opinion: Volume 52, (1912).

Fig. 4.1 Quote from Norvig (2011)

All of the most successful models are 100% based on stochastic models. Hybrid models are found in *question answering* tools. When it comes to specialist tools, all the most successful tools are relying on probabilistic models—whether they deal with *word-sense disambiguation, co-reference resolution, part-of-speech tagging* or *parsing*. It is not for nothing that these tools also create industries that make trillions of dollars in revenue (which, one might say, unfairly, is contrasted with the total amount of money Chomsky's hapless disciples earn). It is, however, where Norvig appears to hang Chomsky by his own petard—as this quote (in full) will demonstrate:

As Norvig pointed out, all these bigrams (Fig. 4.1) were published prior to Chomsky's book. With reference to *lexical priming*, one might speculate whether Chomsky had not come across these, and the unusual word combination had been stuck somewhere subconsciously in his mind until he recycled them for his own purposes. As a further step, rather than for grammaticality, Norvig uses two different models to show that sentence (a) is several thousand times more probable than (b) Also, as Norvig helpfully points out, Chomsky's model can merely tell whether a sentence is (un-)grammatical. The statistical model tells the user that either sentence is highly unusual—information, surely, that is helpful in advancing fluency in a speaker (be they a native or a learner). It does not stop there, either. As an example, the word *quake* is given—described as an intransitive verb.[6] Therefore, within a very narrow definition, the conclusion to be drawn is that (1) "The earth quaked" must be grammatical. By contrast (2) "*It quaked her bowels" is **ungrammatical**.[7] However, the bigram quaked *her* is, indeed found in use as Figure 4.2 shows:

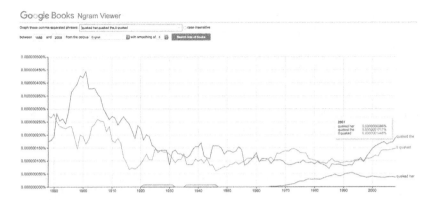

Fig. 4.2 Google books n-gram (checked in January 2018) results for "it quaked" vs "quaked the" and "quaked her" usage

"Quaked her" appears to be, indeed, in use, and it is also a recent development.

It can be claimed that "usage" does not mean grammaticality. However, there are two counter arguments: as Harris and Norvig and others (the lexicographer Patrick Hanks, the corpus linguist John Sinclair, the NLP specialist Chris Manning; Zellig Harris as described above) say: there is the key issue of *likelihood*. "Earth quaked" is a lot more frequently come across than "it quaked"—yet both are deemed grammatical. Figure 4.2 shows that, around ten years ago, "it quaked" was over four times more likely to be found in written books than the transitive ("ungrammatical") "quaked her".[8] There is also an important precedent for this construction:

> Then shook and *quaked the* solid ground: The mountains, from their roots unbound, Mov'd and were shaken: wrath was gone Forth from incens'd Jehovah's throne.

This particular quote comes from *The Book of Psalms* in its 1824 edition. As a result, it can be pointed out that a probabilistic model has no problem with "right" or "wrong" grammar. What can be said that *quake* has a high probability to occur with intransitive usage, while the word's transitive usage is a low probability event.[9] This point has been raised by many, amongst others, by Abney (1996) who declared that "[t]o a significant degree, I think linguistics has lost sight of its original goal, and turned Chomsky's expedient into an end in itself" (Abney 1996: 4).

While we have seen that a number of senior AI researchers have a clear interest in linguistics (Norvig and Pereira, e.g.), there are also those who started as linguists, for example, Steve Abney, who started reading Modern Languages and the Classics and received his PhD in linguistics from MIT in 1987. It was his work at Bell Labs that seemed to have turned him into a computational linguist after that. The CV of Chris Manning is similar: his BA (in 1989) focussed on mathematics, computer science and linguistics. He received his PhD in linguistics at Stanford five years later. He has taught computational linguistics ever since. All four of them describe their encounters with *corpus linguistics*. In fact, Chapter 2 of Manning's hugely influential *Probabilistic Syntax* (2002) is called "The joys and perils of corpus linguistics". Significantly, both Manning (2017) at the start of his Stanford NLP course and Ramisch (2015), in the introduction to his book refer to one of the key pillars of corpus linguistics, namely John Firth's declaration that:

> You shall know a word by the company it keeps. (Firth 1957: 11)

Throughout this book, we have seen a wide range of approaches that keep coming back to this dictum. It has also pointed to the idea of *soft constraints* as Manning (2002) calls them. We can find, therefore, that instead of the "hard constraints" of a well-formed grammar which has syntax as its sole focus, there should be, a lexically driven approach. This, while still carrying imperfections, might, indeed, provide a better model of what "language" is:

> The opportunity to leave behind ill-fitting categorical assumptions, and to better model probabilities of use in syntax is exciting. The existence of 'soft' constraints within the variable output of an individual speaker, of exactly the same kind as the typological syntactic constraints found across languages, makes exploration of probabilistic grammar models compelling. (Manning 2002: 328)

Pointedly, this matches almost fully my own thinking about language, its structure and its usage.

What this shows to us is, that overall, it is not two cultures, two groups of researchers who are each living in their own box that we are dealing with. Yorick Wilks told me, that "AI/NLP people discovered corpora for themselves—they didn't get any message from Sinclair even though he was saying similar things."[10] This hints at a parallel development. However, as demonstrated above, a lot of linguistic background knowledge assisted in making NLP work. In fact, the current crop of AI researchers can be seen as carrying on the task of understanding language which sprung out of traditional linguistics was diverted, far too long, by a Chomskian approach and then got back to be far closer to the natural occurring means of communication with Fillmore's *Construction Grammar* (1988, 2013) and corpus linguistics as pioneered by John Sinclair. In the light of this, it becomes understandable that great minds think alike—and that there is cross-pollination. In the annotated reference list of his 2002 article, Norvig indicated that there has been a magnet-like pull towards those institutions that enable cutting edge research and experiments when it comes to stochastic language modelling. He describes how he remembers giving a talk at Association of Computational Linguists (ACL) on the corpus-based language models used at Google, and Pereira saying to him: "I feel like I'm a particle physicist and you've got the only super-collider" (Norvig 2009). Once Fernando Pereira had got his hands on that super-collider (in other words: the requisite tools to test his theories and build benchmark-grade tools), his ideas of language and language theories clearly evolved. Pereira highlights that linguists are the practitioners of language who have long and deep insight in the matter, awareness of nuances, acres of theory and lifetimes of work to prove it. What used to be a painstaking collection of examples to support a theory can now be done within a relatively short period of time with computational tools. Concordance software sifting through all kinds of text types, texts ancient and new is a case in point. Yet, compared to the resources of the latest crop of technology companies and the kind of access to engineers who can create sophisticated language modelling, university-bound linguists are on the outside, looking in at best. According to Norvig: "[a] few years later he [Pereira] moved to Google. Fernando is also famous for his quote 'The older I get, the further down the Chomsky hierarchy I go'" (ibid.).

I guess (and there lies the author's hope) that this is true for the reader, younger at the start of the book, older now, as well.

4.3   Learning from Linguists: Language Research Areas

4.3.1   Introduction

We saw in Sect. 4.2 the linguistic background (backstory) of a number of key researchers in NLP and AI. There seem to be, however, a number of areas that have had little research time devoted to them amongst AI engineers and developers so far. This section therefore focusses on the fields of research where it can be assumed that linguists can give important, relevant material and insights for a number of languages.

There are obvious issues one has to be aware of: for example, far more often than people realise, teams of researchers tackle similar tasks—yet they are completely unaware of each other simply because they work in different fields. Furthermore, "interdisciplinary research" is often talked about—yet the allocation of funding streams and different research cultures can undermine any such efforts. Another crucial issue is that either inertia or success leads to complacency: what works is merely refined, not questioned and radically overhauled. Thus, for example, the so-called *sugar rush fallacy,* where social media tools have been optimised with the aim of users to spend more time on this site so to maximise advertising revenue. A side effect appears to be that the algorithm recommends ever more extreme views in order to keep the user's attention. The social consequences, however, are ignored even though some detect a definite threat to the fabric of our societies.[11] This is given as the kind of example that must necessarily be relevant for the AI applications described here. Highly sophisticated language processing tools, developed by commercial providers, may have a blind spot for a number of essential factors when it comes to language use. For this reason in particular, the reader is being directed to number of areas where AI developers can, in my opinion, learn from linguists.

4.3.2   Learning from Linguists: Language Research Areas

It is, to my mind, the insights of (corpus) linguists, in a variety of other fields (like *discourse analysis, pragmatics* or *variational linguistics*) where the AI community can find useful sources for further developments. Below are just a few thoughts which have been sketched out. A carefully considered, complete list would require more space than is available here.

- **A is for *aborigines***

Once one starts about language, the complexity (as well as history and politics) of what we see as "language" provokes a great deal of questions. Here are a few that might be considered.

What words of the Australian aborigines are known? Well, there is *kangaroo* for example, boomerang and—what else? Also: did the aborigines write these words down? If so, what system did they use? Or, being now a minority in a country where English is written and spoken—are they transcribing a spoken language into text, using Latin letters and English spelling conventions? Those aborigines are just a case in point: there are a lot of languages out there that only exist in spoken form. Many of these languages are also very different to the Indo-European languages. Obviously, modern recording technologies are a way of capturing a certain amount of spoken languages—which makes the fieldwork of linguists working with such languages a lot easier. It is the of wealth experience, collected over hundreds of years by anthropologists and early linguists, which makes it possible to detect structure and patterns in these languages. This still does not mean that they can all put it into the confines of a sound-based pronunciation transcription (like the IPA), less so into the English alphabet. How, for example, can the *click* languages be transcribed? This, however, points to a problem that every corpus linguist faces, namely *what is a word?* The longer this innocently easy question is being considered, the trickier it becomes to present a definite answer. Is a word the item between two blank spaces, or not? For example, *all together* has formed a single form: *altogether*. Similarly, there are marked semantic difference between a *black bird* and a *blackbird*. Yet one might question why *candlelight* is one word, when *candle-lit* looks like two? Is it *can do* or *can-do*? Clearly, there are rules to apply hyphenation, yet why is it not pen-ultimate. What about fixed idioms like *you know what I mean*? Should it not be written as it is heard spoken, i.e. *younknowhatimean*? Given that English has no ultimate regulatory body when it comes to conventions of the written language, the number of variations is larger than in, say French or German.

- **C is for corpora**

Corpora exist in (at least) four dimensions. One split is between spoken and written texts. Another split is between *specialist corpora* (say, transcripts of all the BBC Reith lectures or all of Dickens' novels) and *general corpora* (which have excerpts of a large variety of text types). The model for the later was the original *Brown Corpus* in the early 1960s. It was deemed to be extremely large, as it consisted of one million words. Corpora in the 1980s (Bank of English, BNC) were then measured as tens of, then hundreds of millions of words. As Norvig noted (see Norvig 2011) trillion-word corpora are now the norm for many AI applications. In Chapter 3, we have shown that corpora used to train the tools tend to be smaller, so as to save computing time (though they are getting, over time, more sophisticated). A common misconception is that the large corpora used by NLP algorithms are all general corpora. WordNet is, for example, not a text corpus: it resembles a huge thesaurus. It also has the disadvantage of being based on relatively old sources (Brown to start with, then material like "Roget's International Thesaurus" (1977). However, the latest comprehensive input was based on COMLEX (1993)).[12] Where this becomes training data, more recent developments and wording choices will end up being ignored.

Where corpora are being used, they could be defined as *general specialist* corpora. For example, the Google *Books* database is probably the largest and most comprehensive corpus of printed books available; it is also the most structured such corpus. With the public n-gram tool, a user can chose specialist sub-corpora for English data (American English, British English and English Literature) as well as a time frame from 1500 to 2009. However, the alternative is to scrape vast amounts of material from the web. While this appears to be a general corpus, it is unstructured and is specialist to a degree in its contents: not all types of text (nor all kinds of writers) are represented on the www space. There are also imbalances with regard to the types of material thus collected. Spoken corpora are hard to obtain and are very time-consuming to transcribe, and material tends to be influenced by the way it was collected. Apparently, Google obtained their training material for their speech recognition and processing tools by allowing volunteers to make free phone calls that it recorded (see Levy 2011). Spoken corpora in made use of in the current academic / publishing setting need to have written consent from the parties recorded.

That individual corpora can diverge to a large degree has been described elsewhere (Pace-Sigge 2013, 2015). A clear advantage of small and specialist corpora created and evaluated by linguists (and that means: mostly "by hand") as opposed to the automatically created vast text corpora is the ability to find nuances and highly relevant distinctions. Sinclair reportedly told corpus linguists to actually have read the material that they put into a corpus. While computer tools enable to make visible what is not spotted by the naked eye, a human reader might notice what is lost to statistical tools. Vaughan and Clancy (2013) demonstrate this with two case studies looking at pragmatic markers in tiny corpora (in the 20,000–50,000-word range). Another example is the research by Egbert and Mahlberg (2017) that shows that the text type (sub-corpus) *fiction* is, indeed, too broad a category. Looking at the novels of Charles Dickens, they split the material into the "spoken" sections (which, indeed, was very close to what a spoken corpus would show) and the remaining text, which is the "narrative part". Based on their investigation, they found the following:

> We show that stark differences between the narrative prose produced by Dickens and his representation of character speech. We also reveal a diachronic change in Dickens's narrative writing style that is not found in his fictional speech, suggesting that this pattern could not have been revealed had we not divided the novels into narrative and speech. Finally, we show that while the narrative-speech distinction is the strongest predictor of linguistic variation.

Such things can easily be missed where the corner stone of all research is size, not direction or quality of the data used.

- **D is for discourse**

Discourse, *discourse analysis* and *critical discourse analysis* are areas that have been widely published about, and this is not the place to document it. Discourse analysts have always used real data as their basis. As Partington et al. (2013) describe that corpus linguistics has added extra material and tools. The subject splits into two broad categories: *spoken discourse* and *written discourse*. The former being, as Jones (2016: 1) "people use conversations to manage their lives". It must be seen in reference to the prosodies occurring in utterances (see, **E**). "Managing lives links" to the performatives described by Austin (1962) in his book *How to do things with words*. Furthermore, there are utterances that are actions—the *speech acts* described by J. R. Searle in 1975. Both the written and the spoken can use a level of non-directness that forces the recipient to "read between the lines". Automatic systems, however, focus on a "bag of words" approach. This means that the machine is able, based on statistical models looking at the co-text, to infer the context. Yet it is a tone-deaf approach that can miss nuances unless there are also lexical signals.

- **E is for EEG measurements**

One might ask why this is relevant—unless language science is used for purposes of healthcare. However, EEG measurements are being used to compare reactions to different kinds of spoken utterances. A recent piece of research traced looked in how far the process of connecting collocation processes can actually be tracked in people's brain activity.

In her PhD thesis, Hughes claims that her experiments

> ... provide sufficient evidence to suggest that there *is* a neurophysiological difference in the way that the brain processes collocational adjective-noun bigrams compared to non-collocational adjective-noun bigrams. I therefore conclude that the phenomenon of collocation *can* be seen as having psychological validity. (Hughes 2018: 269)

Another important feature of language[13] is to be found not in the lexis (the semantic content) but in the actual sound production. English is, in effect, a tonal language. Not tonal in its segmentation (within syllables) but over utterances. Intonation, in spoken utterances, is, indeed a main conveyor of meaning—compared to the actual words (the lexis)— in particular as a speaker starts or ends a turn.[14] *Intonation* has crucial grammatical functions: statements or questions, offers or commands, exclamations or responses, calls, greetings as well as expressing alarm. Intonation reflects mood: it lets the speaker convey aloofness or surprise, anger or fondness, disbelief or sarcasm, etc. Halliday and Greaves (2008) have described all these in their book *Intonation in the Grammar of English*. They concern themselves with a key aspect of phonology, namely *prosody*: the use of intonation and rhythm in order to construe experiential meaning. Intonation features like *pitch, loudness, length* (cf. 41) and the use of (micro-)pauses send signals to the receiver. While modern text-to-speech software is very good in producing a voice that sounds near-natural (unlike the robotic-sounding examples of the past), personal assistants remain rather tone-deaf to prosodic features. These could, however, be integrated through a feedback-loop, in particular for personal assistants worn on one's body (e.g. smart watches). These digital tools already have sensors to produce health-related measurements. Kakouros et al. (forthcoming) have shown that prosodic prominence does affect speakers to a degree that EEG[15] observations can detect these. Furthermore, Kakouros and Räsänen (2016) describe the necessary tool to read prosodic features in their paper "An unsupervised method for the automatic detection of sentence prominence in speech". A more detailed study can be found in Jeff Hanna et al. paper (2017) on whether the mind stores the individual parts of a phrasal verb as a single item or not. They set out with a simple premise: "If particle verbs whose elements appear contiguously are words, we can expect them to be lexical units. What is far from obvious, however, is whether particle verbs which appear in discontinuous form are still analysable as lexical units" (Hanna et al. 2017: 87).[16] In order to see how the mind "sees" and thus processes particle verbs, the authors recruited 31 participants from the student population of the Freie Universität Berlin. These were given four groups of stimuli: "all stimuli used the same verb stem, and contained 700 standard (probability of occurrence = 0.83), and 140 deviant stimuli (probability of occurrence = 0.17)" (Hanna et al. 2017: 90). Their results demonstrate that the sciences of the mind can, indeed, support the concept that is described by John Sinclair as a *lexical item*:

> Our present and previous neurophysiological results sit nicely with this observation, suggesting that the neurobiological mechanisms underlying particle verb processing resemble those of whole from stored constructions – regardless of whether particle and verb appear in canonical or reversed order and regardless of whether they precede each other immediately or materialise as discontinuous constituents. (Hanna et al. 2017: 95)

This is, of course, also relevant with regard to what constitutes a "word"—as a *lexical item* can be a single word though is, more often than not, a set of words.

- **I is for idiosyncrasies**

Idiosyncrasies are, in language, word choices, pronunciation characteristics and certain often-repeated patterns that are specific to one person. It is widely assumed that a person's speech and writing style is as unique as their fingerprint. This fact underpins a lot of work in *forensic linguistics* and *stylistic studies*. It also underpins the science of identifying authors of texts (used, e.g., to determine how much of each of Shakespeare's plays was written by the bard himself; also, to identify plays where he has provided his own material). This "speech fingerprint" is used by some banks as an alternative to traditional passwords and security question for telephone banking. However, electronic "personal assistants" are only personalised based on the history of a person's web search history (or other requests). See also *V is for varieties*.

- **I is for implicature**

This concept is part of *discourse studies*. *Implicature* goes back to the work of Paul Grice (1975) who described a process of inferencing meaning from what we hear.[17] Key to this is the *Cooperative Principle* whereby the speaker and listener aim for a common purpose. Yet, time and again, there seems to be a breach in the four maxims Grice set out: despite this, the listener will understand not what is said but what is implied. A modification has been proposed by the neo-Griceans, Sperber and Wilson, who have reduced the maxims to the one of relation: "Communicators do not 'follow' the principle of relevance: and they could not even if they wanted to. The principle of relevance applies without exceptions" (Sperber and Wilson 1995: 162; as quoted in Archer et al. 2012: 58). Probabilistic language models can predict what word, set of words, or what construction may follow given an initial input. There are strident efforts to create text-summarisation tools (see, Gambhir and Gupta 2017 for an overview). The latest tool by the *Facebook AI Research* unit proposes the use of recurrent *neural networks* (see, Chopra et al. 2016). Still, these systems are blind: they cannot process implicature. *Implicature* is, in this case, linked to what Hoey (2005) calls *semantic association*. Digital tools, however, appear to rely only on surface forms. Tone of voice—even where it is highlighted by lexical choices rather than just intonation patterns—is ignored. Instead, the virtual language comprehender seems to rely on keywords to provide an "answer".

Figure 4.3 demonstrates the author's attempts to provoke *SIRI* to be not her usual reserved self. The first text is a typical example of implicature use: it could be an invitation to have the beverage, it could be an invitation to have a chat, it could mean something more intimate: this all relies on occasion and intonation. SIRI though has been programmed to react to the chunk "you want". This becomes clear where the typical

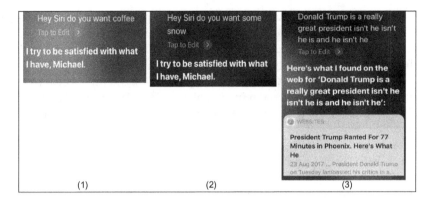

Fig. 4.3 SIRI not understanding implicature

offer (1) is compared to the a-typical, rather nonsensical one in (2) Being non-sentient, SIRI has no wants and needs. The example in (3) was not just tone-deaf to the intonation pattern—the tag question at the end whether in its single form or over-exaggerated as shown is ignored.[18] While such pragmatic markers would render the question as rhetorical or, indeed, ironical SIRI seems to have picked up only surface forms: "Donald Trump" = "President Trump" and repetition = rant. This example shows where linguists, in particular those concerned with pragmatics and also discourse analysis (see below, too) demonstrably understand more than *understanding machines*.

- **P is for politics**

"Language is considered one of the most important means of initiation, synthesizing and *reinforcing* (sic) ways of thinking, feeling and behaviour which are related to the social group" as Basil Bernstein (1971: 63) pointed out in his seminal book *Class, Codes and Control*. If we understand language as a cultural artefact of humanity, the glue that binds people together; if we see language as a means to express and also directs thoughts and feelings than implications of using language in interaction with digital tools cannot and must not be ignored.[19]

In themselves, computers cannot be biased. However, they can only ever be as neutral as the input material they have. It has to be remembered that their training material has been chosen by researchers that are fully human—and humans carry their own personal values and stereotypes into these selections, whether they are aware of it or not.[20] This has to be acknowledged: "Don't overlook the inherent subjectivity of building things with data just because you're using math", as data scientist Fred Benenson says in an interview with Tyler Woods (2016).[21] All of this stands in sharp contrast to the research presented by decades of critical discourse analysis.

- **T is for translation**

Above, we have seen the strident efforts and improvements made to create a machine-based translation tool. Despite the oddities and inadvertently funny translations such digital tools may present, the improvements seen over just the last decade are nothing but not impressive. Still, while demonstration translations seem to be close to the human translator's benchmark, everyday usage still falls short of expectations. Nevertheless, electronic translations are helpful and cost-effective when it comes to shorter texts where the recipient needs to know the content rather than a fully precise translation. Furthermore, one approach machines use is to see whether there is an already existing translation to match it. There are, however, clear reasons why human translators will not lose their jobs. One is the area of legal documents and interpretation within the legal justice system. Given the importance to give a precise and accurate representation of what has been written or said (also: to have the ability to directly check), human translators will still be necessary. The other area is the translation of books, or, to be more precise, imaginary texts (poetry and prose). The element of cultural references and values writers reflect would be difficult to instil into a machine. Furthermore, authors tend to employ "transferred meaning elements" (metaphors and the like). While a machine should be able to recognise and translate fossilised and highly frequent forms, neologisms and newly created metaphorical elements which need to be translated into an appropriate target-language equivalent would be above the pay scale of a robot translator. Another, crucial, issue is the translation into and from minority languages. Despite its considerable scope *Google Translate* still only produces laughable results where Finnish to/from English is concerned.[22]

However, as the use of parallel corpora has already become typical of a translator's set of tools, machine-assisted translation will certainly

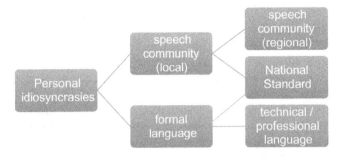

Fig. 4.4 Possible variations of a person's spoken language

help drafting translations, making the process faster and, dare we say it, cheaper. Still: given that many publishers pay a fixed sum, such computer-aided translations should create the space to concentrate on the trickier and often more beautiful parts of the original.

- **V is for varieties**

Language has divergence within convergence (otherwise, there would be a breakdown of communication). It is, at the moment, left to linguists to describe the many variations found. Where AI uses speech recognition, for example speech that displays a strong regional accent can lead to hilarious results.

Figure 4.4 demonstrates how a single person might use different variants of the same language. Within the local speech community, there might be further differentiations (say, between neighbours, friends and family). *Formal Language* might be used for all kinds of encounters with superiors or officials; *technical or professional language* is in reference to specific terminology and change of register (if, say the person is a lecturer...).

Another point is that language changes—imperceptibly but constantly. This means that training material, over time, starts becoming less useful.

- **W is for World Englishes**

A major drawback of language work done by major corporations is that they reflect a bias towards their home market (typically the US of A) and, where they go beyond the variant of American English, tend to focus on the so-called *core* English speaking countries, namely Australia, Britain, Canada, Eire and New Zealand. However, outer core countries (India, Nigeria, Pakistan, Singapore, etc.) have taken ownership of English in their own ways and there are highly relevant differences. Moreover, English is also the *lingua franca* of business, technology, culture (in some respects), etc.: as such, more people speak English as a second language than as a first language. There is a wide body of scholarship—both traditional linguistics and, increasingly, corpus-based—that takes account of this. For example, one of the earliest collections of English spoken around the world (where it an official language) is the International Corpus of English (ICE), which is run under the auspices of University College London. On the NLP and AI side, however, it is rarely the developers that try and create tools for working with these variants.[23] Clearly, this is one area where scholars are far ahead of engineers.

4.3.3   Learning from Linguists: Hapax Legomena/Rare Words

Hapax Legomena (or, for short, *hapax*, also referred to as *rare words*) are one of the most interesting areas of language. However, they are also one of the trickier fields to study. This term refers to words which occur only once in a single text. The frequency curve of words in any given text or collection of texts (corpus) follows Zipf's description; that is, very few words (usually grammatical ones like *articles, prepositions* etc.) are highly frequent, some are mid-range, a substantial number of words occur only once.[24] This gives a pretty good idea how relevant hapaxes are. It also highlights why this is an issue for statistical language processing tools: *rare words* are often ignored, binned or left unaccounted for. Yet this seems to contradict the aim of building language understanding—it does not help to only focus on the high-frequency quartile of (lexical) words in the input but ignore rare words which, counted together, make up a substantial part of any text or collection of texts.

Renouf and Bauer point out that, even back in 1970, a study by Gleitman and Gleitman "illustrate the difficulties that speakers can have in interpreting novel words (in that case compounds) when no context is provided to support an interpretation" (Renouf and Bauer 2001: 232). As a result, the authors refer to Baayen and Neijt's "contextual anchoring" that allows the listener or reader to come up with a suitable interpretation of words Renouf had classified during her earlier research (cf. Renouf and Bauer 2001: 233). These include most prominently:

- new referents to real-world phenomena
- words created in the making of linguistic jokes phenomena
- words constructed for the purposes of lexical cohesion
- rare words like archaisms and revivals
- orthographic/typographic variation
- solid compound previously hyphenated or vice versa
- rare plural forms

Renouf and Bauer describe that in a written text a writer can provide overt "conscious help"—using punctuation, glosses or explanatory phrases; or covert "unconscious help"—where the context aids disambiguation. They list techniques like *forms of repetition, collocation* (where the recipient's expectations assist), *semantical relation* (like synonyms or antonyms, etc.), *parallelism*, the *lexical field* as well as *pragmatical markers*. It should be added that there can be both an overlap and a number of such "helpers" employed. Crucially, the text type or genre is highly relevant. Renouf and Bauer highlight that, as their research was based on newspaper texts, the amount of neologisms might be higher. They found only 2.5% of the hapaxes had overt markers. The most successful approach to disambiguate, according to them, is *morphological analysis* as (at least in newspaper material) *compoundisation* appears to be the most frequent form of creating new words. *Hapaxes* have been used to conduct style analysis, notably to discover authorship—see, for example, Ali and Hussein (2014).[25]

In the area of NLP, hapax legomena clearly pose a problem. Statistical models work with high-frequency items, whereas everything below a cut-off point is usually discarded. Instead, engineers have created a placeholder commonly referred to as *UNK*:

> Because computing high dimensional softmax is computationally expensive, in practice the shortlist is limited to have only top- K most frequent words in the training corpus. All other words are then replaced by a special word, called the **unk**nown word (UNK). (Gulcehre et al. 2016, author's highlights)

Thus, there is the *rare word problem* as any kind of training corpus is bound to miss out on any relevant rare words—and these are often carrying relevant information within each sentence. One idea to avoid having the holes that an UNK would create is to have a list of rare words (see Luong et al. 2014). The issue with hapax legomena is, however, that no list can be suitably comprehensive enough. We have seen in Chapter 3 (e.g. Jozefowicz et al. 2016) that LSTM techniques are providing the best-performing computational techniques to deal with rare words. NLP engineers have also realised that hapaxes are very useful when it comes to machine translations. Sennrich et al. (2015) highlight that rare words should be given extra weighting "[s]ince rare words tend to carry central information in a sentence". Hapaxes help with alignment in translations—see, for example, Lardilleux and Yves Lepage (2007). Luong and Manning (2016) describe a number of ways to deal with rare words, using *deep recurrent character-level models* and which is even outperforming complex morphological analysers. And yet: when compared to the multitude in which hapax legomena have been found to be realised (as demonstrated by Renouf and Bauer nearly twenty years ago), all the attempts to build probabilistic language modelling tools appear to fall far too short to deal with a key element of language as it occurs in daily usage.

4.4   THE STRUCTURE OF LANGUAGE

This book is concerned with two key issues. One, in how far there are common roots and overlaps between linguists and AI language model developers and, two, whether direct applications[26] can be seen as validating certain theories of language structure. Harold Palmer ([1938] 1961) had given an outline of a *pattern grammar* as early as the 1930s and his colleague, Albert Hornby, published the seminal *A Guide to Pattern and Usage in English* in 1954. These can be seen as a precursor to Fillmore's *Construction Grammar*; the idea of *pattern grammar* was updated with corpus-based material by Hunston and Francis (1999). In the meantime, Wittgenstein and, in particular, J. R. Firth had stressed the point that any given word does not carry meaning in itself but obtains its meaning from the context it is found in—a notion that, to some degree, can also be found in the early works of Zellig Harris. However, it was the TGG, with its idea of an innate universal human grammar ability that, since the later 1950s (and, in some places, up to this day), determined the discussion, teaching and views of language. Ross Quillian briefly hinted at a AI project which tried to use a TGG model—yet got nowhere.

Were we to say that the proof that a theory is correct lies in the successful application of said theory, then, crucially, the probabilistic approach to language appears to be the most valid so far. Where digital tools can recognise, understand and process language inputs and produce almost human-like outputs, we seem to have a model that mimics natural processes to a high degree. It has to be remembered that people like Minsky or Quillian tried to replicate neural networks in electronic form; that psychologists, all the way back to the 1960s, tried to see human minds as mere Bayesian *probabilistic information processing systems*. One has to take into consideration that work by Tversky and Kahnemann (1973) gave strong indications that the human mind computes probabilities all the time, a concept that has found yet more validation in more recent research. At the same time, AI engineers construct "neural networks" and "long short-term memories", thus continuing to mimic brain functions. Looking at the level of language comprehension a speech-directed virtual personal assistant demonstrates, it appears that the AI engineers have cracked it: grammar, indeed, is not some abstract, fixed, inbuilt construct. Rather, it is a bag of words, very lexically-led and the relations individual words or word chunks have to each other are highly probabilistic.

Admittedly, AI solutions work best for spoken language as it relies a lot on pre-constructed chunks.[27] Because of the nature of spoken English, it is (relatively speaking) easier to have a predictive system: the kind of probabilistic algorithm behind personal assistants. This high-level predictability also enables these systems to deal fairly well with individual variations in sound production.

In this context, it has to be always remembered that Ross M. Quillian did not only want to produce a machine—everything points towards the second aim of producing a "model of language": his theories were therefore not just meant to be a blueprint for engineers. They were, very importantly, also aimed to create a linguistic theory how language functions.

Nevertheless, the application of a probabilistic grammar model holds also true for written texts. This is a valid claim even when one considers that published written texts (as opposed to informal forms of writing: personal letters, social media or mobile media entries) are less natural: writers demand of themselves that their language is of a higher, more refined standard; publishers will recommend and ask for changes. As a result, these written texts are more of an artifice than an informal or spoken product: these texts go through redrafting sessions; these texts might be the product of more than one writer.[28] This does not mean that artificial language models cannot deal with these. It does mean, however, that it faces greater obstacles and achieves a lower success rate overall.

Nevertheless: in both its spoken and its written form, a probabilistic system, focussing on the *lexis*—how words stand in relation to each other as J. R. Firth would say—appears to be the answer to the question "what is grammar?".

NOTES

1. In 2001, Tim Berners-Lee and colleagues expanded the notion of a Semantic *Web* even further: "The Semantic Web will bring structure to the meaningful content of Web pages, creating an environment where software agents roaming from page to page can readily carry out sophisticated tasks for users". In: Berners-Lee, T., Hendler, J., and Lassila, O. 2001. The Semantic Web. *Scientific American*, 284(5), 28–37.
2. In *Stanford Encyclopaedia of Philosophy*. "Alan Turing". https://plato.stanford.edu/entries/turing/ (last accessed 12/2017).
3. Wilks (1985) raises a similar criticism, speaking of the "wrongheadedness of Chomsky's preoccupation with syntax and semantics-based methods to understand language".
4. In *Syntactic Structures*, he wrote "I think we are forced to conclude that … probabilistic models give no particular insight into some of the basic problems of syntactic structure".
5. In corpus linguistics, any text input would be referred to as *text*—regardless whether the source is written or spoken. In phonetics and related fields, the spoken "text" would be referred to as an *utterance* whereas engineers (both electrical engineers and engineers in the digital field refer to *signals*).
6. The example seems to have been taken from Wilson and McEnery (2001) *Corpus Linguistics: An Introduction*. University of Edinburgh Press. See also Atkins and Levin (1995) discussion of *quake* and *quiver*. http://www.lancaster.ac.uk/fss/courses/ling/corpus/Corpus4/4LEX2.HTM (last accessed 12/2017).
7. In his 1995 novel, *It Might Have Been Jerusalem*, Thomas Healy uses the phrase "it quaked her bowls".
8. It is interesting to note that "quaked her" appears to be a fixed phrase. Yet the same construction, saying either "quaked it" or "quaked him", return zero results in the Google n-gram viewer.
9. John Sinclair in the Collins COBUILD English Grammar (1990) and Rosamond Moon (1998) point out that certain words tend to monopolise a particular grammatical construction and, therefore, certain collocational sets are idiomatic, even if they could be seen as "ungrammatical" by some. The young computational linguist Carlos Ramisch (2015) describes with simple examples how Chomsky's approach is having clear repercussions

when trying to create an NLP application: "In the traditional generative grammatical framework, the representation of idioms poses a
challenge" (24).

10. Personal communication (via e-mail, November 2017).

11. This refers to research undertaken by Guillaume Chaslot on the algorithm of *YouTube* recommendations. https://algotransparency.org/. This
has been discussed in the British *Guardian* newspaper (https://www.
theguardian.com/technology/2018/feb/02/youtube-algorithm-elec-
tion-clinton-trump-guillaume-chaslot) and a month later in the *New York
Times* (https://www.nytimes.com/2018/03/10/opinion/sunday/you-
tube-politics-radical.html). See also the paper by the relevant developers:
Deep Neural Networks for YouTube recommendations (Covington et al.
2016). https://static.googleusercontent.com/media/research.google.
com/en//pubs/archive/45530.pdf (all last accessed 03/2018).

12. See the WordNet site of Princeton University. https://wordnet.prince-
ton.edu/wordnet/frequently-asked-questions/database/ (last accessed
12/2017).

13. I cannot, of course, speak for all languages. This particular issue will be
discussed here in relation to English.

14. This is described, in detail, in Pace-Sigge (2017).

15. Electroencephalography—measurements of electric activity in the brain.

16. The target language in this experiment was German, yet similar results can
be expected with regard to, for example, English *phrasal verbs*.

17. A personal priming could be the rhyme hear-ear and the connection to
this poem: A rabbit's ears are made of plush / And lined with lovely pink;
They tell him when he ought to rush / Or when to stop and think (May
Carlton Lord).

18. Even where the question is straightforward rather than exaggerated
("Donald Trump is a great president, isn't he?"), SIRI gives the same
answer.

19. Awareness must, indeed, go beyond the spoken word. Barfield (2015)
describes the latest innovations in brain-to-computer interfaces. He
describes that there are early results that resemble telepathy (brain-to-brain
communication). Indeed, there have been (fuzzy so far) results in brain-to-
computer and brain-to-AI communication. A person was shown a picture
of a person and the computer, measuring brainwaves, could, albeit only in a
rough form, recreate a "picture showing person" image. Indeed, Facebook
engineers claimed that, in future, users do not need to click the "like" button but simply thinking it will allow the machine to "like" an entry.

20. Non-awareness appears to be the norm as encounters with facial recognition software appears to show: these tools have greater difficulty with
female faces (as most engineers are male) and there have been cases where

African-American people have been categorised as "ape"—again, the lack of black faces in the engineering community has created a deep hole in the training data.

21. Further reading on these issues can be found here. https://www.socialcooling.com/ and http://www.mathwashing.com (last accessed 12/2017).

22. One might raise the question as to *what* the Finns have to say that is of interest in the world. (*Finns* here is the stand-in for speakers of any language spoken by only relatively small speech-communities). However, the inverse is seen as true: What does the world *miss* when a Finnish speaker is not heard? It might, after all, that somebody who has not acquired English (or Spanish, French, etc.) has something to tell that is hugely relevant to a large number of non-Finnish speakers. (Though I cannot supply evidence for this claim, it might be just a particular ideology.)

23. To indicate how papers or training packages are being marketed it can be found that in many cases where "English as a Lingua Franca" is described, one potential use for it is NLP.

24. Cartoni (2006) describes that 40% of a corpus consists of hapaxes.

25. It is debatable, however, whether it can be deemed sufficient to provide conclusive answers, in particular when compared to the large range of probabilistic tools available—as demonstrated by, for example, Grieve (2007).

26. The "trillion-dollar industry" Norvig referred to in a quote in 4.2.2.

27. As has been described by John Sinclair, Alison Wray and others— see Pace-Sigge (2013) for details. In fact, this insight harks back to work done by G. A. Miller (1956) to which both I and Peter Norvig refer to.

28. There might be a reason, however, why journalism has a high degree of clichés usage, namely deadlines. If only a relatively short time is available to draft and revise a text, writers will have to fall back on the known, tried and tested (to use a cliché).

REFERENCES

Abney, Steve. 1996. Statistical Methods and Linguistics. In *The Balancing Act: Combining Symbolic and Statistical Approaches to Language*, ed. Judith L. Klavans and Philip Resnik. Cambridge: MIT Press.

Ali, Sundus Muhsin, and Khalid Shakir Hussein. 2014. The Comparative Power of "Type/Token" and "Hapax Legomena/Type" Ratios: A Corpus-Based Study of Authorial Differentiation. *Advances in Language and Literary Studies* 5 (3): 112–119.

Archer, Dawn, Karin Aijmer, and Anne Wichman. 2012. *Pragmatics: An Advanced Resource Book for Students*. London: Routledge.

Austin, J.L. 1962 [2001]. *How to Do Things with Words*. Oxford: Oxford University Press.

Barfield, Woodrow. 2015. *Cyber-Humans Our Future with Machines*. Cham: Springer.

Bernstein, Basil. [1971] 1973. *Class, Codes and Control*. St. Albans: Paladin.

Cartoni, Bruno. 2006. Constance et variabilité de lincomplétude lexicale. In *Proceedings of TALN/RECITAL 2006*, 661–669. Leuven, Belgium.

Chomsky, N. 1965. *Aspects of the Theory of Syntax*. Cambridge, MA: MIT Press.

Chopra, Sumit, Michael Auli, and Alexander M. Rush. 2016. Abstractive Sentence Summarization with Attentive Recurrent Neural Networks. In *Proceedings of the 2016 Conference of the North American Chapter of the Association for Computational Linguistics: Human Language Technologies*, 93–98.

Covington, Paul., Adams, Jay, and Sargin, Emre. 2016. Deep Neural Networks for YouTube Recommendations. In *Proceedings of the 10th ACM Conference on Recommender Systems*, 191–198. ACM.

Egbert, Jesse, and Michaela Mahlberg. 2017. *Fiction—One Register or Two? Narrative and Fictional Speech in Dickens' Novels*. Presentation, Corpus Linguistics 2017, Birmingham. Long abstract at: https://www.birmingham. ac.uk/Documents/college-artslaw/corpus/conference-archives/2017/general/paper323.pdf. Last Accessed 12/2017.

Fillmore, Charles J. 1988. The Mechanisms of "Construction Grammar". *Annual Meeting of the Berkeley Linguistics Society* 14: 35–55.

Fillmore, Charles J. 2013. Berkeley Construction Grammar. In *The Oxford Handbook of Construction Grammar*, ed. Thomas Hoffmann and Graeme Trousdale. Oxford: Oxford University Press.

Firth, John R. 1957. *Papers in Linguistics 1934–1951*. London: Oxford University Press.

Gambhir, Mahak, and Vishal Gupta. 2017. Recent Automatic Text Summarization Techniques: A Survey. *Artificial Intelligence Review* 47 (1): 1–66.

Grice, H. P. 1975. Logic and Conversation. In *Syntax and Semantics*, eds. P. Cole and J. Morgan, vol. 9. New York: Academic Press.

Grieve, Jack. 2007. Quantitative Authorship Attribution: An Evaluation of Techniques. *Literary and Linguistic Computing* 22 (3): 251–270.

Gulcehre, Caglar, Sungjin Ahn, Ramesh Nallapati, Bowen Zhou, and Yoshua Bengio. 2016. Pointing the Unknown Words. *arXiv preprint* arXiv:1603.08148.

Halliday, M.A.K., and William S. Greaves. 2008. *Intonation in the Grammar of English*. London: Equinox.

Hanna, Jeff, Bert Cappelle, and Friedemann Pulvermüller. 2017. Spread the Word: MMN Brain Response Reveals Whole-Form Access of Discontinuous Particle Verbs. *Brain and Language* 175: 86–98.

Harris, Zellig S. 2002. The Structure of Science Information. *Journal of Biomedical Informatics* 35: 215–221.

Hoey, Michael. 2005. *Lexical Priming*. London: Routledge.

Hornby, Albert S. 1954. *A Guide to Pattern and Usage in English*. London: Oxford University Press.

Hughes, Jennifer. 2018. *The Psychological Validity of Collocation: Evidence from Event-Related Brain Potentials*. Unpublished PhD thesis, ESRC Centre for Corpus Approaches to Social Science. Department of Linguistics and English Language, Lancaster University.

Hunston, Susan, and Gill Francis. 1999. *Pattern Grammar a Corpus-Driven Approach to the Lexical Grammar of English*. Amsterdam: John Benjamins.

Jones, Rodney H. 2016. *Spoken Discourse*. London: Bloomsbury.

Jozefowicz, Rafal, Oriol Vinyals, Mike Schuster, Noam Shazeer, and Yonghui Wu. 2016. Exploring the Limits of Language Modeling. *arXiv preprint* arXiv:1602.02410.

Kakouros, Sofoklis, Nelli Salminen, and Okko Räsänen. 2018. Making Predictable Unpredictable with Style—Behavioral and Electrophysiological Evidence for the Critical Role of Prosodic Expectations in the Perception of Prominence in Speech. *Neuropsychologia* 109: 181–199.

Kakouros, Sofoklis, and Okko Räsänen. 2016. 3PRO—An Unsupervised Method for the Automatic Detection of Sentence Prominence in Speech. *Speech Communication* 82: 67–84.

Lardilleux, Adrien, and Yves Lepage. 2007. The Contribution of the Notion of Hapax Legomena to Word Alignment. In *Proceedings of the 4th Language and Technology Conference (LTC07)*, 458–462.

Levy, Steven. 2011. *In the Plex: How Google Thinks, Works and Shapes Our Lives*. New York: Simon and Schuster.

Luong, Minh-Thang, and Christopher D. Manning. 2016. Achieving Open Vocabulary Neural Machine Translation with Hybrid Word-Character Models. *arXiv preprint* arXiv:1604.00788.

Luong, Minh-Thang, Ilya Sutskever, Quoc V. Le, Oriol Vinyals, and Wojciech Zaremba. 2014. Addressing the Rare Word Problem in Neural Machine Translation. *arXiv preprint* arXiv:1410.8206.

Manning, Christopher. 2002. Probabilistic Syntax. In *Probabilistic Linguistics*, ed. Rens Bod, Jennifer Hay, and Stefanie Jannedy, 289–341. Cambridge: MIT Press.

Manning, Christopher (with Richard Socher). 2017. Natural Language Processing with Deep Learning CS224n/Ling284. Lecture 11. Stanford University.

Miller, George A. 1956. The Magical Number Seven, Plus or Minus Two: Some Limits on Our Capacity for Processing Information. *Psychological Review* 63 (2): 81–97.

Moon, Rosamond. 1998. *Fixed Expressions and Idioms in English: A Corpus-Based Approach.* Oxford: Oxford University Press.

Norvig, Peter. 2009. Natural Language Corpus Data. In *Beautiful Data*, ed. T. Segaran and J. Hammerbacher, 219–242. Boston, MA: O'Reilly.

Norvig, Peter. 2011. Colorless Green Ideas Learn Furiously: Chomsky and the Two Cultures of Statistical Learning. *Significance* 9 (4): 30–33. http://norvig.com/chomsky.html. Last Accessed 12/2017. Short version 2012.

Pace-Sigge, Michael. 2013. *Lexical Priming in Spoken English.* Basingstoke: Palgrave Macmillan.

Pace-Sigge, Michael. 2015. *The Function of TO and OF in Multi-word Units.* Basingstoke: Palgrave Macmillan.

Pace-Sigge, Michael. 2017. Can Lexical Priming Be Detected in Conversation Turn-Taking Strategies? In *Lexical Priming: Applications and Advances*, ed. M. Pace-Sigge and K.J. Patterson, 93–120 Amsterdam: John Benjamins.

Palmer, Harold E. [1938] 1961. *A Grammar of English Words.* London: Longman, Green.

Partington, Alan, Alison Duguid, and Charlotte Taylor. 2013. *Patterns and Meaning in Discourse. Theory and Practice in Corpus-Assisted Discourse Studies (CADS).* Amsterdam and Philadelphia: John Benjamins.

Pereira, Fernando. 2000. Formal Grammar and Information Theory: Together Again? *Philosophical Transactions of the Royal Society of London A: Mathematical, Physical and Engineering Sciences* 358 (1769): 1239–1253.

Quillian, M. Ross. 1966. *Semantic Memory.* Unpublished Doctoral Dissertation, Carnegie Institute of Technology (Reprinted in Part in M. Minsky (Ed.), *Semantic Information Processing.* Cambridge: MIT Press, 1968).

Quillian, M. Ross. 1969. The Teachable Language Comprehender: A Simulation Program and Theory of Language. *Computational Linguistics* 12 (8) (August): 459–476.

Ramisch, Carlos. 2015. *Multiword Expressions Acquisition: A Generic and Open Framework.* Cham: Springer.

Renouf, Antoinette, and Laurie Bauer. 2001. Contextual Clues to Word-Meaning. *International Journal of Corpus Linguistics* 5 (2): 231–258. Amsterdam and Philadelphia: John Benjamin.

Russell, Stuart, and Peter Norvig. 2005. *Artificial Intelligence: A Modern Approach*, 3rd ed. Englewood Cliffs, NJ: Prentice-Hall.

Sennrich, Rico, Barry Haddow, and Alexandra Birch. 2015. Neural Machine Translation of Rare Words with Subword Units. *arXiv preprint* arXiv:1508.07909.

Shanker, Stuart G. 1987. Wittgenstein Versus Turing on the Nature of Church's Thesis in Special Issue on Churchs Thesis. *Notre Dame Journal of Formal Logic* 28 (4): 615–649.

Sperber, Dan, and Wilson, Deidre. 1995. *Relevance: Communication and Cognition.*

Tversky, Amos, and Daniel Kahneman. 1973. Availability: A Heuristic for Judging Frequency and Probability. *Cognitive Psychology* 5 (2): 207–232.

Vaughan, E., and B. Clancy. 2013. Small Corpora and Pragmatics. *The Yearbook of Corpus Linguistics and Pragmatics* 1: 53–73.

Wilks, Yorick. 1985. *Bad Metaphors, Chomsky and Artificial Intelligence.* Computing Research Laboratory, New Mexico State University.

Woods, Tyler. 2016. Mathwashing, Facebook and the Zeitgeist of Data Worship. *Technically Brooklyn*, June 8. Available at https://technical.ly/brooklyn/2016/06/08/fred-benenson-mathwashing-facebook-data-worship/. Last Accessed 12/2017.

CHAPTER 5

Conclusions

Abstract The book is completed with a short conclusion which will consolidate some of the key points made throughout the earlier chapters. Not unlike the history of technological development, insights into the processes that have let speakers understand and produce language as well as tools that mimic these processes have advanced with increasing speed over the last century. In fact, the neuron-network inspired concepts were already described by Quillian in 1961. It is unsurprising that his work is referred to both by those who create digital tools of artificial intelligence and those who try to explain how human language works. Now, in 2018 it is time for AI specialists and linguists to compare notes and see where the other has come up with answers for their problems.

Keywords Quillian · Spreading activation · AI · Linguistics

Not unlike the history of technological development, insights into the processes that have let speakers understand and produce language as well as tools that mimic these processes have advanced with increasing speed over the last century.

In that time, what had been mere theoretical frameworks outlined by Church, Turing and also Wittgenstein served as a basis for ambitious projects. In an age where computational machines were first developed and built, Marvin Minsky already tried to copy the neurological set-up

© The Author(s) 2018
M. Pace-Sigge, *Spreading Activation,*
Lexical Priming and the Semantic Web,
https://doi.org/10.1007/978-3-319-90719-2_5

of the human brain. The result was the first *neural network computer*, simulating a network of several dozen neurons. The good news was that the early enthusiasm (certainly driven by unreasonable expectations) was not crushed by the prevailing realities. In the 1950s and 1960s, computers (and therefore, access to computing time) were few and far between; even relatively simple computational tasks required machines that filled rooms—Large ones. Given the environment of 2018, it becomes truly difficult to comprehend that the facilities available to so many of us now are only the result of very recent achievements in design and development. It must be critically noted that a lot of the technology has been developed through funding by the US taxpayer via defence projects. At the end of the day, many of the crucial technologies and algorithms were only developed in the 1980s and 1990s.[1]

One of the still very theoretical, neuron-network inspired concepts for a twentieth century mechanical Turk was described by M. Ross Quillian (1961) and developed over the next decade. His aim was to create a *Teachable Language Comprehender* (1969). With this, he introduced the concept of *priming*: the potentiation of a node (a word) by having been linked to another node or series of nodes previously. The overarching concept is the firing-up of the neural network that is the human brain: in a machine, that is *spreading activation*. Tellingly, Quillian referred to this as "a simulation program"—that is, a programme that can be taught to "understand" (in other words, *process*) language; crucially, however, it was also meant to be a "theory of language". This means that Quillian himself did not restrict his theoretical model to the field of computational science but also saw it as discussion how language itself functions. While Quillian left the field of AI research, the key elements of his research certainly live on. *Spreading Activation* assumes that information is stored in the form of a semantic network. Consequently, to train such a network, input can be specific to the task—Quillian gives the example of feeding twenty stories that deal with "firefighters" to enable the machine to understand the concept. This example highlights a crucial issue: semantic knowledge. Collins and Quillian (1972) realised as much when they tried to make spreading activation conform to a tree-like model of various concepts: these two could not be brought to combine to a satisfying degree. It was also a key criticism raised by Peter Norvig (1987). One solution had been touched upon (though not elaborated on) by Quillian: constraints. Once the model is put into a suitable frame (genre, text-type, exchange-type specific) the number of possible nodes activated would be reduced. For example, the word "expansion" has a different semantic network where if used as

1. common parlance as compared to
2. usage amongst economists or,
3. in a text book on astrophysics.

This notwithstanding, the *theory of language* indicated by Quillian was found to be demonstrable. The information retrieval model described gave an insight how words stand in relation to each other and how frequent co-occurrence can spread activate nodes in concert. That *spreading activation* facilitates (or inhibits) a process of retrieving the next node has been demonstrated by Meyer and Schvaneveldt (1971); and then, in more detail, by James Neely (1976). Like Collins and Quillian, these investigations looked at participant's reaction time between *linked, non-linked* and impossible (*non-word*) combinations. This became, until sophisticated EEG and MRI scans were employed, the best method to make spreading activation patterns in a human brain visible. Neely referred to the process as *semantic priming of the lexical memory*, thus combining the process of priming with the idea that this is lodged in a (subconscious) for of **lexical** memory.

It was another three decades, however, until Michael Hoey (2005) used the concept to create his theory of *lexical priming* in order to explain the phenomena that corpus linguistics had described, namely *collocation, colligation and semantic association* (*semantic prosody*). As such, *lexical priming* functions like a bridge between a general understanding of how language is organised in people's minds and how (repeat) exposure shapes people's (subconsciously employed) word-usage patterns. To be a tool of functioning communication, language must be a platform that has a large degree of commonality: the words, idioms, structures and associations that are understood by the vast majority of speakers. Yet, as any speaker acquires language, certain primings will be stronger than other ones[2]—they will have been encountered in contexts (some may only be known in a spoken rather than a written environment) that are personal to each language user. Certain dispreferences may likewise be the result of personal primings: a language user will not have come across particular constructions and therefore hesitate to use them themselves.[3] Hoey also described how primings can be broken (usually for creative or humorous effect). Such diversions from what is expected will only be understood, however, if the recipient is aware of the wider framework such breaches take place in.

The language description provided by the lexical priming theory (cf. Hoey 2005) has been found to be very similar to the approach used to apply probabilistic models for speech recognition and text understanding software. Here the degree of priming is mapped via vector space models. Trained on ever larger data sets, these algorithms have a probability equivalent to a listener's/speaker's expectation. Chapter 3 describes in detail how the challenge to construct a machine *language comprehender* has been approached theoretically and practically and how the results achieved have become increasingly more impressive. Nevertheless, software developers and AI engineers have to balance the desire to provide the perfect system with the need to minimise computational cost. We have seen that, for example, a *real world model* would take a lot more processing time and capacity. Furthermore, it would treat all paths equally—which is not efficient. Using a *small world model* and a reduced set of training vocabulary may, however, produce a number of noticeable gaps when it comes to process input. As has been demonstrated in the chapter, enormous efforts have been (and are being) made to make these language understanders more nimble and proficient. In fact, the last decade in particular has seen the first stage of maturity in NLP tools which are now widely found in mobile devices (SIRI, Google Go, Google Assistant and Google Translate) and voice-activated AI devices in the home (Amazon's Alexa), in cars and indeed, the factory floor.[4] It has to be noted, too, that the development of this technology is still very young and further breakthroughs can be expected.[5]

We have seen, in Sect. 4.2, that a lot of NLP and AI developers either have their roots in linguistics (like Chris Manning) or have some deep linguistic training (like Peter Norvig or Fernando Pereia). It is not that corpus linguists came knocking and said "hey, you engineers, look at those corpora we have got…". Still, many key AI researchers will have been aware of developments or have looked for research in the field of linguistics to find research that would back up their own work.[6]

It is quite true what Pereia said: that he works in the field, yet it is tech giants like Google who have access to all the tools his research would require to support his theories fully. Section 4.3 shows that there are still suitably large white areas on the map of language modelling technology that are being addressed by linguists but which has received not enough attention yet by the AI crowd. In fact, one could say that there is still a lot engineers can learn from many decades of investigations into language production and reception.

Finally, Sect. 4.4, crucially, presented an important insight for linguists: namely, that a theory is more likely to be right if it can be applied, replicated and if it can show workable results. This book has argued that, as a result, a probabilistic model that puts *lexis* in the foreground and that subordinates structural patterns ('grammar') to a word-driven model of language appears a more accurate representation of human language than a theory of some kind of "innate grammar".

NOTES

1. Just as a reminder of the most recent time-line. Computers could recognise and read out text documents in the 1980s (the Apple Macintosh had text-to-speech engine called MacinTalk in 1984). IBM launched its voice-recognition software, *ViaVoice*, in 1997. Google, then merely a search engine, was first launched in the late 1990s, incorporated as a company in 1998. SIRI, the digital personal assistant was first developed in 2005 and became integrated in Apple products (who bought the company who had created the system) since 2010. It was, however, Amazon's *Alexa* which seemed to have made personal virtual assistants ubiquitous. Alexa was launched in 2014.

2. Indeed, as the majority of speakers on this planet grow up bi- or multilingual, many speakers will retain parallel primings in their head (thus, e.g., linking FIRE! to both *firemen* and *bomberos*).

3. I remember that a colleague of my mother's once said "I know that the past perfect tense exists. But I don't know what it means and I never use it myself".

4. I deliberately say "first stage" here: the technology is still in its early stages and "first stage" merely refers to the fact that it is only now that the technology has started to become widely available, starts being implemented and has become a focal point for economists and in politics. See, also, this impact assessment by the *World Economic Forum*: https://www.weforum.org/agenda/2017/12/advancements-in-ai-are-rewriting-our-entire-economy/ (last accessed 12/2017).

5. As shown in Chapter 3, this has already happened during the work on this book. *Google Duplex* was presented on the 8th of May 2018. This system can operate fully autonomously, though it is restricted to a tightly pre-scriped domain (service-encounters) at the time of writing. One can only speculate on the impact fully functioning high-spec quantum computing would have: a technology that has the possibility to speed up current calculation processes enormously.

6. Yorick Wilkes (personal communication) described how he or Roger Schank would do work that was very similar to Charles Fillmore's—and then quote him for the approach they took.

REFERENCES

Collins, Allan M., and M. Ross Quillian. 1972. Experiments on Semantic Memory and Language Comprehension. In *Cognition in Learning and Memory*, ed. L.W. Gregg, 117–137. New York: Wiley.

Hoey, Michael. 2005. *Lexical Priming: A New Theory of Words and Language*. London: Routledge.

Meyer, David E., and Roger W. Schvaneveldt. 1971. Facilitation in Recognizing Pairs of Words: Evidence of a Dependence Between Retrieval Operations. *Journal of Experimental Psychology* 90 (2): 227–234.

Neely, James H. 1976. Semantic Priming and Retrieval from Lexical Memory: Evidence for Facilitatory and Inhibitory Processes. *Memory and Cognition* 4 (5): 648–654.

Norvig, Peter. 1987. *A Unified Theory of Inference for Text Understanding*. PhD Thesis, University of California, Berkeley.

Quillian, M. Ross. 1961. The Elements of Human Meaning: A Design for and Understanding Machine. *Communications of the ACM* 4 (9): 406–418.

Quillian, M. Ross. 1969. The Teachable Language Comprehender: A Simulation Program and Theory of Language. *Computational Linguistics* 12 (8): 459–476.

Bibliography: Further Reading

Early AI

Brunner, J.S. 1955. *A Study of Thinking.* New York: Wiley.

Charniak, Eugene. 1972. *Toward a Model of Childrens Story Comprehension,* AI-Tech, Rep-266. Cambridge: MIT AI Labs.

Edwards, Ward. 1962. Dynamic Decision Theory and Probabilistic Information Processings. *Human Factors* 4 (2): 59–74.

Miller, George A. 1956. The Magical Number Seven, Plus or Minus Two: Some Limits on Our Capacity for Processing Information. *Psychological Review* 63 (2): 81–97.

Minsky, Marvin L. 1952. *A Neural-Analogue Calculator Based upon a Probability Model of Reinforcement.* Cambridge, MA: Harvard University Psychological Laboratories.

Minsky, Marvin L. 1958. Some Methods of Artificial Intelligence and Heuristic Programming. In *Proceedings of the Symposium on the Mechanization of Thought Processes,* Teddington.

Shanker, Stuart. 1987. Wittgenstein Versus Turing on the Nature of Churchs Thesis in Special Issue on Churchs Thesis. *Notre Dame Journal of Formal Logic* 28 (4): 615–649.

Shanker, Stuart. 1995. Turing and the Origins of AI. *Philosophia Mathematica* 3 (1): 52–85.

Simmons, Robert. 1963. Synthetic Language Behaviour. *Data Processing Manager* 5 (12): 11–18.

Turing, Alan M. 1937a. On Computable Numbers, with an Application to the Enscheidungsproblem. *Proceedings of the London Mathematical Society* 2 (42): 230–265.

© The Editor(s) (if applicable) and The Author(s) 2018   121
M. Pace-Sigge, *Spreading Activation,*
Lexical Priming and the Semantic Web,
https://doi.org/10.1007/978-3-319-90719-2

Turing, Alan M. 1937b. Computability and λ-Definability. *The Journal of Symbolic Logic 2* (4): 153–163.

Turing, Alan M. 1950. Computing Machinery and Intelligence. *Mind, New Series* 59 (1236): 433–460.

Wilensky, Robert. 1983. Memory and Inference. In *International Joint Conference on Artificial Intelligence (IJCAI)*, August, 402–404.

Wilks, Yorick. 1973. *Preference Semantics* (No. STAN-CS-73-377). Department of Computer Science, Stanford University.

Wittgenstein, Ludwig. 1953 [1949]. *Philosophical Investigations*. Oxford: Basil Blackwell.

SEMANTIC WEB, SPREADING ACTIVATION AND PRIMING

Bell, A., and M.R. Quillian. 1969. *Capturing Concepts in a Semantic Net* (No. Scientific-13), Bolt Beranek and Newman Inc., Cambridge, MA.

Berners-Lee, T., J. Hendler, and O. Lassila. 2001. The Semantic Web. *Scientific American* 284 (5): 28–37.

Collins, Allan M., and Elizabeth F. Loftus. 1975. A Spreading-Activation Theory of Semantic Processing. *Psychological Review* 82 (6): 407–428.

Collins, Allan M., and M. Ross Quillian. 1970. Facilitating Retrieval from Semantic Memory: The Effect of Repeating Part of an Inference. *Acta Psychologica* 33: 304–314.

Collins, Allan M., and M. Ross Quillian. 1972a. Experiments on Semantic Memory and Language Comprehension. In *Cognition in Learning and Memory*, ed. L.W. Gregg, 117–137. New York: Wiley.

Collins, Allan M., and M. Ross Quillian. 1972b. How to Make a Language User. In *Organisation of Memory*, ed. E. Tulving and W. Donaldson, 319–322. New York: Academic Press.

Collins, Allan M., E.H. Warnock, N. Aiello, and M.L. Miller. 1975. Reasoning from Incomplete Knowledge. In *Representation and Understanding: Studies in Cognitive Science*, ed. D.G. Bobrow and A. Collins. New York: Academic Press.

de Groot, A.M.B., A.J.W.M. Thomassen, and P.T.W. Hudson. 1982. Associative Facilitation of Word Recognition as Measured from a Neutral Prime. *Memory and Cognition* 10: 358–370.

Habib, Reza. 2001. On the Relation Between Conceptual Priming, Neural Priming and Novelty Assessment. *Scandinavian Journal of Psychology* 42: 187–195.

Harrington, Brian. 2010. A Semantic Network Approach to Measuring Relatedness. In *Proceedings of the 23rd International Conference on Computational Linguistics: Posters*, 356–364.

Jurafsky, Dan, and James H. Martin. 2014 [2000]. *Speech and Language Processing*. London: Pearson.

Kahneman, David. 2011. *Thinking Fast and Slow*. New York: Farrar, Straus and Giroux.

Klein, B., L. Cosmides, J. Tooby, and S. Chance. 2001. Priming Exceptions: A Test of the Scope Hypothesis in Naturalistic Trait Judgements. *Social Cognition* 19 (4): 443–468.

Loftus, Elizabeth F. 1973a. Activation of Semantic Memory. *American Journal of Psychology* 86: 331–337.

Loftus, Elizabeth F. 1973b. Category Dominance, Instance Dominance, and Categorization Time. *Journal of Experimental Psychology* 97: 70–74.

Loftus, Elizabeth F., and W. Cole. 1974. Retrieving Attribute and Name Information from Semantic Memory. *Journal of Experimental Psychology* 102: 1116–1122.

Loftus, G.R., and E.F. Loftus. 1974. The Influence of One Memory Retrieval on a Subsequent Memory Retrieval. *Memory and Cognition* 2: 467–471.

McCulloch, Warren S., and Walter Pitts. 1943. A Logical Calculus of the Ideas Immanent in Nervous Activity. *The Bulletin of Mathematical Biophysics* 5 (4): 115–133.

McDonald, S.A., and R.C. Shillcock. 2003. Eye Movements Reveal the On-Line Computation of Lexical Probabilities During Reading. *Psychological Science* 14 (6): 648–652.

Meyer, David E. 1970. On the Representation and Retrieval of Stored Semantic Information. *Cognitive Psychology* 1: 242–300.

Meyer, David E. 1973. Correlated Operations in Searching Stored Semantic Categories. *Journal of Experimental Psychology* 99: 124–133.

Meyer, David E., and R.W. Schvaneveldt. 1976. Meaning, Memory Structure and Mental Processes. *Science* 192 (April 2): 27–33.

Meyer, David E., and R.W. Schvaneveldt. 1984. Discussion of Meyer, David E., and R.W. Schvaneveldt. 1971. Facilitation in Recognizing Pairs of Words: Evidence of a Dependence Between Retrieval Operations 1971. *Citation Classic* 47 (November 19).

Neely, James H. 1976. Semantic Priming and Retrieval from Lexical Memory: Evidence for Facilitatory and Inhibitory Processes. *Memory and Cognition* 4 (5): 648–654.

Neely, James H. 1977. Semantic Priming and Retrieval from Lexical Memory: Roles of Inhibitionless Spreading Activation and Limited-Capacity Attention. *Journal of Experimental Psychology General* 106: 226–254.

Paul, Stephen T., and George Kellas. 2004. A Time Course View of Sentence Priming Effects. *Journal of Psycholinguistic Research* 33 (5) (September): 383–405.

Prucha, Jan. 1972. Psycholinguistics and Sociolinguistics—Separated or Integrated. *Linguistics* 89 (89): 9–23.

Quillian, M. Ross. 1961. The Elements of Human Meaning: A Design for and Understanding Machine. *Communications of the ACM* 4 (9) (September): 406.

Quillian, M. Ross. 1962. A Revised Design for an Understanding Machine. *Mechanical Translation* 7: 17–29.

Quillian, M. Ross. 1967. Word Concepts: A Theory and Simulation of Some Basic Semantic Capabilities. *Behavioral Science* 12: 410–430.

Quillian, M. Ross. 1969. The Teachable Language Comprehender: A Simulation Program and Theory of Language. *Computational Linguistics* 12 (8) (August): 459–476.

Ratcliff, Roger, and Gail McKoon. 1988. A Retrieval Theory of Priming in Memory. *Psychological Review* 95: 385–408.

Saller, Harald. 2004. Zugriff auf Wissen, Zugang zum Sinn. Anmerkungen zu Texten, Kommentaren und sematischen Netzen. In *PhiN-Beiheft* 2/2004, 66–82.

Sherman, Steven J., Matthew T. Crawford, David L. Hamilton, and Leonel Garcia-Marques. 2003. Social Inference and Social Memory: The Interplay Between Systems. In *The SAGE Handbook of Social Psychology*, ed. Michael Hogg and Joel Cooper, 45–67. London: Sage.

Titchener, E.B. 1922. A Note on Wundts Doctrine of Creative Synthesis. *The American Journal of Psychology* 33 (3): 351–360.

Traxler, M., D. Foss, R. Seely, B. Kaup, and R.K. Morris. 2000. Priming in Sentence Processing: Intralexical Spreading Activation, Schemas and Situation Models. *Journal of Psycholinguistic Research* 29 (6): 581–595.

Trofimovich, Pavel. 2005. Spoken-Word Processing in Native and Second Languages: An Investigation of Auditory Word Priming. *Applied Psycholinguistics* 26: 479–504.

Whitney, Paul. 1998. *The Psychology of Language*. Boston and New York: Houghton Mifflin Company.

Williams, J.N. 1996. Is Automatic Priming Semantic? *European Journal of Cognitive Psychology* 8: 113–161.

CORPUS LINGUISTICS AND LEXICAL PRIMING

Angell, James Rowland. 1896. Review of *Outlines of Psychology* by Oswald Külpe. *The Philosophical Review* 5 (4): 417–421.

Biber, Douglas. 2009. A Corpus-Driven Approach to Formulaic Language in English: Multi-word Patterns in Speech and Writing. *Presentation, Corpus Linguistics, 2009 Conference*. University of Liverpool.

Biber, Douglas, Susan Conrad, and Randi Reppen. 1998. *Corpus Linguistics*. Cambridge: Cambridge University Press.

Biber, Douglas, Stig Johansson, Geoffrey Leech, Susan Conrad, Edward Finegan, and Randolph Quirk. 2000. *Longman Grammar of Spoken and Written English*. Harlow: Pearson Education.

Carbonell, J.R., and A.M. Collins. 1973. Natural Semantics in Artificial Intelligence. In *Proceedings of the Third International Joint Conference on Artificial Intelligence*, 344–351.

Castner, Joanna E. 2007. Semantic and Affective Priming as a Function of Stimulation of the Subthalamic Nucleus in Parkinsons Disease. *Brain* 130: 1395–1407.

Cleland, A.A., and M.J. Pickering. 2003. The Use of Lexical and Syntactical Information in Language Production: Evidence from the Priming of Noun-Phrase Structure. *Journal of Memory and Language* 49: 214–230.

De Goede, Dieuwke. 2006. *Verbs in Spoken Sentence Processing: Unravelling the Activation Pattern of the Matrix Verb Pattern of the Matrix Verb*. PhD Thesis, University of Groningen. http://irs.ub.rug.nl/ppn/298832666. Last Accessed 12/2017.

de Groot, A.M.B. 1989. Representational Aspects of Word Imageability and Word Frequency as Assessed Through Word Association. *Journal of Experimental Psychology: Learning, Memory and Cognition* 15: 824–845.

de Mornay Davies, Paul. 1998. Automatic Semantic Priming: The Contribution of Lexical- and Semantic-Level Processes. *European Journal of Cognitive Psychology* 10 (4): 389–412.

Desmet, T., and M. Declercq. 2006. Cross-Linguistic Priming of Syntactic Hierarchical Configuration Information. *Journal of Memory and Language* 54 (4): 610–632.

Ellis, Nick, E. Frey, and I. Jalkanen. 2006a. The Psycholinguistic Reality of Collocation and Semantic Prosody. *Presentation: Exploring the Lexis-Grammar Interface*, Hanover, Germany, 5–7 October.

Ellis, Nick, R. Simpson-Vlach, and C. Maynard. 2006b. The Processing of Formulas in Native and L2 Speakers Psycholinguistic and Corpus Determinants. *Presentation: Exploring the Lexis-Grammar Interface*, Hanover, Germany, 5–7 October.

Ellis, Nick, E. Frey, and I. Jalkanen. 2018, Forthcoming. The Psycholinguistic Reality of Collocation and Semantic Prosody (1): Lexical Access. In *Exploring the Lexis-Grammar Interface. Studies in Corpus Linguistics*, ed. U. Römer and R. Schulze. Amsterdam: John Benjamins.

Gagné, Christina L. 2001. Relation and Lexical Priming During the Interpretation of Noun-Noun Combinations. *Journal of Experimental Psychology* 27 (1): 236–254.

Gobet, Fernand, Peter C.R. Lane, Steve Croker, Peter C.H. Cheng, Gary Jones, Iain Oliver, and Julian M. Pine. 2001. Chunking Mechanisms in Human Learning. *Trends in Cognitive Sciences* 5 (6) (June): 236–243.

Gries, Stefan Th. 2005. Syntactic Priming: A Corpus-Based Approach. *Journal of Psycholinguistic Research* 34 (4): 365–399.

Hoey, Michael. 1991. *Patterns of Lexis in Text*. Oxford: Oxford University Press.

Hoey, Michael. 1995. The Lexical Nature of Intertextuality: A Preliminary Study. In *Organization in Discourse: Proceedings from the Turku Conference*, ed. B. Warvik, S. Tanskanen, and R. Hiltunen, 73–94. Anglicana Turkuensia 14.

Hoey, Michael. 2003. Why Grammar Is Beyond Belief. In *Belgian Essays on Language and Literature*: Belgian Association of Anglicists in Higher Education, 183–196, University of Liège.

Hoey, Michael. 2004a. Textual Colligation: A Special Kind of Lexical Priming. *Advances in Corpus Linguistics* 49: 169–194.

Hoey, Michael. 2004b. The Textual Priming of Lexis. In *Corpora and Language Learners*, ed. S. Bernardini and D. Stewart, 21–41. Amsterdam: John Benjamins.

Hoey, Michael. 2004c. Lexical Priming and the Properties of Text. In *Corpora and Discourse*, ed. A. Partington, J. Morley, and L. Haarman. Bern: PeterLang.

Hoey, Michael. 2008a. Lexical Priming and Literary Creativity. In *Text, Discourse and Corpora*, ed. M. Hoey, M. Mahlberg, M. Stubbs, and W. Teubert, 7–30. London: Continuum.

Hoey, Michael. 2008b. Grammatical Creativity: A Corpus Perspective. In *Text, Discourse and Corpora*, ed. M. Hoey, M. Mahlberg, M. Stubbs, and W. Teubert, 31–56. London: Continuum.

Hoey, Michael, and Matthew Brook O'Donnell. 2008. The Beginning of Something Important: Corpus Evidence on the Text Beginnings of Hard News Stories. In *Corpus Linguistics, Computer Tools, and Applications—State of the Art*, 189–212. Bern: Peter Lang.

Ledoux, Kerry, Christine Camblin, Tamara Y. Swaab, and Peter C. Gordon. 2006. Reading Words in Discourse: The Modulation of Lexical Priming Effects by Message-Level Context. *Behavioral and Cognitive Neuroscience Reviews* 5 (3): 107–127.

Novick, J., A. Kim, and J. Trueswell. 2003. Studying the Grammatical Aspects of Word Recognition: Lexical Priming, Parsing and Syntactic Ambiguity Resolution. *Journal of Psycholinguistic Research* 32 (1): 57–75.

Otten, Marte, Van Berkum, and J.A. Jos. 2008. Discourse-Based Word Anticipation During Language Processing: Prediction or Priming? *Discourse Processes* 45 (6): 464–496.

Pace-Sigge, Michael. 2013. *Lexical Priming in Spoken English Usage*. Houndmills, Basingstoke: Palgrave Macmillan.

Patterson, Katie J. 2016. The Analysis of Metaphor: To What Extent Can the Theory of Lexical Priming Help Our Understanding of Metaphor Usage and Comprehension? *Journal of Psycholinguistic Research* 45 (2): 237–258.

Renouf, A., and J.M. Sinclair. 1991. Collocational Frameworks in English. In *English Corpus Linguistics*, ed. K. Aijmer and B. Altenberg, 128–143. London: Longman.

Scarborough, Don L., Charles Cortese, and Hollis S. Scarborough. 1977. Frequency and Repetition Effects in Lexical Memory. *Journal of Experimental Psychology: Human Perception and Performance* 3 (1): 117.

Scarborough, Don L., Linda Gerad, and Charles Cortese. 1979. Accessing Lexical Memory: The Transfer of Word Repetition Effects Across Task and Modality. *Memory and Cognition* 7 (1): 3–12.

Sinclair, John M. 1987. The Nature of the Evidence. In *Looking Up*, ed. J. Sinclair, 150–159. London: Collins.

Sinclair, John M. 1991. *Corpus, Concordance, Collocation*. Oxford: Oxford University Press.

Underwood, G., N. Schmitt, and A. Galpin. 2004. The Eyes Have It: An Eye-Movement Study into the Processing of Formulaic Sequences. In *Formulaic Sequences: Acquisition, Processing, and Use*, ed. N. Schmitt, 153–172. Amsterdam: John Benjamins.

Whitsitt, S. 2005. A Critique of the Concept of Semantic Prosody. *International Journal of Corpus Linguistics* 10 (3): 283–305.

Wray, Alison. 2002a. *Formulaic Language and the Lexicon*. Cambridge: Cambridge University Press.

Wray, Alison. 2002b. Formulaic Language in Computer-Supported Communication: Theory Meets Reality. *Language Awareness* 11 (2) (October): 114–131.

Wundt, Wilhelm Max. 1862. *Beiträge zur Theorie der Sinneswahrnehmung*. Leipzig und Heidelberg: Wintersche Verlagsbuchhandlung.

Xioa, Richard, and Tony McEnery. 2006. Collocation, Semantic Prosody, and Near Synonymy: A Cross-Linguistic Perspective. *Applied Linguistics* 27 (1): 103–129.

Zimmermann, H.H. 1972. Zur Konzeption der automatischen Lemmatisierung von Texten. In *SFB 100 "Elektronische Sprachforschung": Aspekte d. automatischen Lemmatisierung*. Bericht 10–72. Linguistische Arbeiten 12, 4–10.

ENGLISH LANGUAGE, LEXICOGRAPHY AND LINGUISTICS

Aitchinson, Jean. 1989. *The Articulate Mammal*. London: Routledge.

Archer, Dawn, Karin Aijmer, and Anne Wichman. 2012. *Pragmatics: An Advanced Resource Book for Students*. London: Routledge.

Atkins, Sue, Michael Rundell, and Hiroaki Sato. 2003. The Contribution of Framenet to Practical Lexicography. *International Journal of Lexicography* 16 (3): 333–357.

Austin, J.L. 2001 [1962]. *How to Do Things with Words*. Oxford: Oxford University Press.

Baker, Paul. 2006. *Using Corpora in Discourse Analysis*. London: Continuum.

Gleitman, Lila R., and Henry Gleitman. 1970. *Phrase and Paraphrase: Some Innovative Uses of Language*. New York: W. W. Norton.

Goldberg, Adele E. 1995. *A Construction Grammar Approach to Argument Structure*. Chicago: University of Chicago Press.

Halliday, M.A.K. 1959. *Language of the Chinese "Secret History of the Mongols"*. London: Longman.

Halliday, M.A.K., and R. Hasan. 1976. *Cohesion in English*. London: Longman.

Harris, Zellig S. 2002. The Structure of Science Information. *Journal of Biomedical Informatics* 35: 215–221.

Louw, Bill. 1993. Irony in the Text or Insincerity in the Writer? The Diagnostic Potential of Semantic Prosodies. In *Text and Technology*, ed. M. Baker, G. Francis, and E. Tognini-Bonelli, 157–176. Amsterdam: Benjamins.

Marconi, Diego. 1997. *Lexical Competence*. Cambridge: MIT Press.

Nelson, M. 2000. *The Methodological Background: British Traditions of Text Analysis, Correlative Register Analysis and Corpus Linguistics*. Unpublished PhD Thesis. http://users.utu.fi/micnel/thesis/Chapter5%20.html. Last Accessed 01/2018.

Peters, Ann M. 1983. *The Units of Language Acquisition*. Cambridge: Cambridge University Press.

Wolfram, Walt. 1978. Contrastive Linguistics and Social Lectology. *Language Learning* 28 (1): 1–28.

CURRENT AI DEVELOPMENTS

Canhasi, Ercan. 2016. GSolver: Artificial Solver of Word Association Game. In *ICT Innovations 2015*, ed. Suzana Loshkovska and Saso Koceski, 49–57. Cham: Springer.

Carroll, Glenn, and Eugene Charniak. 1991. A Probabilistic Analysis of Marker-Passing Techniques for Plan-Recognition. In *Proceedings of the Seventh Conference on Uncertainty in Artificial Intelligence*, August, 69–76. Morgan Kaufmann Publishers Inc.

Charniak, Eugene. 1986. A Neat Theory of Marker Passing. *Association for the Advancement of Artificial Intelligence (AAAI)*, 584–588.

Charniak, Eugene, and Robert Goldman. 1988. A Logic for Semantic Interpretation. In *Proceedings of the 26th Annual Meeting on Association for Computational Linguistics*, 87–94. Association for Computational Linguistics.

Chen, Yun-Nung, William Yang Wang, and Alexander I. Rudnicky. 2014. Leveraging Frame Semantics and Distributional Semantics for Unsupervised Semantic Slot Induction in Spoken Dialogue Systems. *Spoken Language Technology Workshop (SLT)*, 584–589. IEEE.

Cheng, P. C.-H., and R. Ananya. 2006. A Temporal Signal Reveals Chunk Structure in the Writing of Word Phrases. In *Proceedings of the Twenty Eighth Annual Conference of the Cognitive Science Society.* Mahwah, NJ: Lawrence Erlbaum.

Clark, Stephen. 2015. Vector Space Models of Lexical Meaning. In *Handbook of Contemporary Semantic Theory*, ed. Shalom Lappin and Chris Fox, 493–522. New York: Wiley.

Conklin, K., and N. Schmitt. 2008. Formulaic Sequences: Are They Processed More Quickly Than Nonformulaic Language by Native and Nonnative Speakers? *Applied Linguistics* 29 (1): 72–89.

Conrad, C. 1972. Cognitive Economy in Semantic Memory. *Journal of Experimental Psychology* 92: 149–154.

Corneli, Joseph, and Miriam Corneli. 2016. Teaching Natural Language to Computers. *arXiv preprint* arXiv:1604.08781.

Damavandi, Babak, Shankar Kumar, Noam Shazeer, and Antoine Bruguier. 2016. Nn-Grams: Unifying Neural Network and N-Gram Language Models for Speech Recognition. *arXiv preprint* arXiv:1606.07470.

Dunietz, Jesse, and Daniel Gillick. 2014. A New Entity Salience Task with Millions of Training Examples. *European Chapter of the Association for Computational Linguistics (EACL)* 14: 205–211.

Grigorev, Alexey. 2017. Vector Space Models. *MLWIKI.* Available at: http://mlwiki.org/index.php/Vector_Space_Models. Last Accessed 11/2017.

Heck, Larry, and Hongzhao Huang. 2014. Deep Learning of Knowledge Graph Embeddings for Semantic Parsing of Twitter Dialogs. *Signal and Information Processing (GlobalSIP), IEEE Global Conference*, August, 597–601.

Hernamdez, A., C. Fennema-Notestine, C. Urdell, and E. Bates. 2001. Lexical and Sentential Priming in Competition: Implications for Two-Stage Theories of Lexical Access. *Applied Psycholinguistics* 22: 191–215.

Hobbs, Jerry R., Mark Stickel, Paul Martin, and Douglas Edwards. 1988. Interpretation as Abduction. In *Proceedings of the 26th Annual Meeting on Association for Computational Linguistics*, 95–103. Association for Computational Linguistics.

Levy, Steven. 2011. *In the Plex: How Google Thinks, Works and Shapes Our Lives.* New York: Simon & Schuster.

Manin, Yuri I., and Matilde Marcolli. 2016. Semantic Spaces. *Mathematics in Computer Science* 10 (4): 459–477.

Manning, Chris (with Richard Socher). 2017. Natural Language Processing with Deep Learning CS224N/Ling284. Lecture 11, Stanford University.

Norvig, Peter. 1983. Six Problems for Story Understanders. *Association for the Advancement of Artificial Intelligence (AAAI)*, August, 284–287.

Norvig, Peter 1988. Multiple Simultaneous Interpretations of Ambiguous Sentences. *Program of the Tenth Annual Conference of the Cognitive Science Society*, August.

Norvig, Peter. 1989. Building a Large Lexicon with Lexical Network Theory. *Proceedings of the IJCAI Workshop on Lexical Acquisition*, August.

Och, Franz Josef, and Hermann Ney. 2003. A Systematic Comparison of Various Statistical Alignment Models. *Computational Linguistics* 29: 19–51.

Prabhavalkar, Rohit, Raziel Alvarez, Carolina Parada, Preetum Nakkiran, and Tara N. Sainath. 2015. Automatic Gain Control and Multi-style Training for Robust Small-Footprint Keyword Spotting with Deep Neural Networks. *Acoustics, Speech and Signal Processing (ICASSP), 2015 IEEE International Conference*, 4704–4708.

Russell, Stuart, and Peter Norvig. 2005. *Artificial Intelligence: A Modern Approach*, 3rd ed. Englewood Cliffs, NJ: Prentice-Hall.

Sinclair, John M. and Mauranen, Anna. 2006. Linear unit grammar: Integrating speech and writing. John Benjamins Publishing.

Wegner, Peter, and Dina Goldin. 2003. Computation Beyond Turing Machines. *Communications of the ACM* 46 (4): 100–102.

Weiss, David, Chris Alberti, Michael Collins, and Slav Petrov. 2015. Structured Training for Neural Network Transition-Based Parsing. *arXiv preprint* arXiv:1506.06158.

Yahya, Mohamed, Steven Whang, Rahul Gupta, and Alon Y. Halevy. 2014. ReNoun: Fact Extraction for Nominal Attributes. *Empirical Methods in Natural Language Processing (EMNLP)*, 325–335.

Yu, Yeong-Ho, and Robert F. Simmons. 1988. Constrained Marker Passing. Artificial Intelligence Laboratory, University of Texas at Austin.

INDEX

© The Editor(s) (if applicable) and The Author(s) 2018
M. Pace-Sigge, *Spreading Activation,*
Lexical Priming and the Semantic Web,
https://doi.org/10.1007/978-3-319-90719-2

GPSR Compliance
The European Union's (EU) General Product Safety Regulation (GPSR) is a set
of rules that requires consumer products to be safe and our obligations to
ensure this.

If you have any concerns about our products, you can contact us on

ProductSafety@springernature.com

In case Publisher is established outside the EU, the EU authorized
representative is:

Springer Nature Customer Service Center GmbH
Europaplatz 3
69115 Heidelberg, Germany